Never forget that we only get rainbows
after we've lived through the rain

Life & Rhymes

Poetry that reflects the ups and downs of life

By Natalie Carr

Published by

Athena's Bounty

Life & Rhymes at Athena's Bounty

Cover design by Natalie Carr through Canva
Illustrations from Canva

Email enquiries: enquiry@athenasbounty.co.uk

ISBN 978-1-7393194-0-3

For Susanne, Emma and Samantha

Women that despite the hardships they've faced, still
endure and inspire me to do the same!

INTRODUCTION

Pleasure to "meet" your acquaintance and welcome to my very first full collection of poems that I'm sharing with the world!

I'm Natalie, a child of the 90s, with two children who have inspired me to fulfil my dreams so I can show them that they can achieve anything they set their mind to. I started writing poetry when I was nine years old after being gifted a Flower Fairies library. I fell in love with poetry after that and couldn't stop writing for family and friends, poems about my dog, my fish, what was happening at school....

It wasn't until I began my business Athena's Bounty in 2019 that I started to share my poetry outside of my immediate circle. I have written poems for customer's wedding days, anniversaries, birthdays and thank yous. I have written poems in memory of lost family members and to express how important and special people were to each other. I have wanted to publish a book since forever, but was always a little too scared to share everything with everyone. Then I decided that I wasn't going to hide anymore and here I am...a Disney mad, Netflix obsessed girl who loves singing, dancing (badly), anything musical theatre and writing.

Why is poetry so important to me?

Poetry has always been a way to express the inner and darkest aspects of myself. What I'm really thinking and feeling. There is something so cathartic about writing it all down. Some choose journaling, I chose poetry. I always thought that these poems couldn't be shared, like how you wouldn't publish your diary. Then, I realised, after sharing some of my darker poems, that people could see themselves within my words. I wasn't alone and they weren't alone either! In that moment of sharing, we realised we don't only have to share the sunshine and rainbows aspects of ourselves; we can be real and raw. This book is as up and down as life is. From the highest of highs to the lowest of lows. This book is all of me and I would like to finally introduce myself to you all...

What I want this book to be for you...

Poetry or creative writing in general is a fantastic way of collating all your thoughts and feelings and sorting through them all. Its like having a clear-out of your head. It allows you to challenge thoughts and feelings you have. It gives you a medium in which to share those thoughts and feelings with others so that they can better understand you and how to possibly help you too.

Use these poems to prompt your own writing and for anyone saying, oh but I can't write....says who? When you first entered this world there were so many things that you "couldn't do", you just couldn't do them yet. Small steps can lead to large victories, but before that can happen you have to make the choice to take that first small step. Your first step is picking up a pen/pencil, grabbing a piece of paper and extracting the words from your mind.

Chapters

This Book is split into four sections:
Standing in Shadows reflect poems from when I was at my lowest. Struggling to find a way out of the darkness.

Phoenix Rising are poems to uplift. A lot of these poems were written when I had started my journey into improving my mental health and had finally sought help for my struggles.

Blood, S*** and Tears are all poems about motherhood. From those first thoughts and feelings to dealing with sleep deprivation, tantrums and everything in between.

Social Lessons is what it says on the tin. Lessons that I have learnt throughout my life interacting with people. Lessons that I want to make sure get a voice so we can try and improve things. There are poems that touch on bullying, sexual misconduct and our reliance on social media for validation.

CONTENTS

BLOOD S*** AND TEARS 179

SOCIAL LESSONS   245

LIFE AND RHYMES

Life and rhymes, rhymes and life,
Of being a mother and being a wife.
The struggles of depression, the struggles of weight,
The struggles of always putting too much on my plate.
The balancing act, the perfectionist,
Feeling like I've been wading through thick mist.
Seeing clearer, clearly seeing,
That letting go of my stress can be so freeing.
Sharing that journey, with those in my hole,
I'm freeing myself, now lets free your soul.

STANDING
IN
SHADOWS

STANDING IN SHADOWS

My own mental health has always been a little more up and down than I would have liked. I always felt that I was fighting this invisible battle from within, that often came out through my writing. The poems in this chapter are very raw and emotive. There are poems that tackle what depression looks and feels like, struggles with self image, and controlling relationships. So disclaimer time; if you are at a low point in your own mental health I advise to read these with someone else present. It may help to read the words to someone so they can understand how you feel if your words reflect my own. It's important that when we are feeling this way and want to be left alone in our depression, that we are not. Isolation is the oxygen that depression needs.

If you are feeling like you need help or support with your depression or low mood then there are lots of people who are there to offer their support and guidance. At the back of this book I will include some of the service providers available that can help, along with some techniques I have picked up on my own mental health journey.

You will notice as the chapter continues, the poems get lighter and more positive which I hope will take you on that journey as well if you are struggling at this moment.

"Poetry is a journey through the ebb and flow of the mind; where words have the power to connect, empower and reveal"
Natalie Carr

OPEN YOUR EYES

Written 2003, age 13

Open your eyes,
What do you see?
An incomplete picture,
Showing me.
I don't feel happy,
I don't feel whole,
I feel like a girl without my soul.

It feels like I've been swept away,
To another week,
To another day.
Time has stopped,
Or is getting slower,
It's never finished,
It's never over.

I'm really mixed up,
All inside.
I tried to run away,
I tried to hide.
It did not work,
I am still here.
I wish that I,
Could just disappear.

In loving memory of

LIESCHEN STRECKER

22ND DECEMBER 2007-
14TH DECEMBER 2022

This next poem was my tribute to a lost youth. This for me highlights why mental health awareness, kindness and love are so important, as we just don't know how much someone may need it.

ODE TO A LOST TEEN

My heart is breaking,
The absence aching,
Your departure feels so final.
Why did you leave me?
You never believed me,
But you aided my survival.

You gave me purpose,
You brought such love,
Even with a mind so tortured.
Your beautiful soul,
Your energy boundless,
I'm sorry you felt so cornered.

I know there was nothing more,
That I could do or say,
That could take away the pain inside,
To make you feel okay.

And although my heart is breaking,
With the aching absence of you,
I hope you have found the peace,
You deserved your whole life through.

I know it feels so final,
But I must remember it is not.
For even a gaping wound
Can be sealed by a stitch and knot.

To seal the goodness in,
And take comfort in our memories,
We immortalise each one of them,
And turn them into treasuries.
For you are not really gone my sweet child,
You live on forever in my heart,
And although your body has gone,
Our souls will never be apart.

What we must remember is, broken things can often be put back together again with love and care!

BROKEN

Everything inside is broken,
Although it has a smile on its face.
The pieces all smashed together,
Inside its perfectly intact case.

Its engine coughs and splutters,
Running out of gas,
Waiting for this struggle and strife
To finally come to pass.

No one stops to check,
What's happening inside.
When it comes to things such as this,
Negativity is easy to hide.

For no one wants to see it,
They like it locked behind,
A shiny smooth exterior,
Which allows them to be blind.

"I didn't know what was happening,
I didn't know how bad,
I just thought that it was a phase,
They just seemed a little sad".

Don't lock it all away,
And don't turn a blind eye,
Cause the last thing you really want,
Is to be standing in front of a gravestone asking why.

It can be difficult to let go of what we find familiar. Even if it is bad for us.

COMPANION

I want to die,
Yet I'm afraid of death,
Wanting something to change,
But unsure of the steps.
Everything seems black,
Like I'm buried underground,
With the weight on top of me,
I can feel it pound by pound.
It crushes all my hope,
It drowns out all the light,
It makes me feel so isolated,
With no possible end in sight.
But then someone comes along,
And tries to set me free,
They take some of the pressure off,
They let me know,
They see me.
They offer out a hand to hold,
I have to be ready to take it,
But so many times it's happened before,
I've chosen to dwell in my pit.
Why can't I take that hand?
Why can't I finally be free?
Because this feeling is all I've known,
My companion is misery.

We cope in the ways we know how,
until we learn better ways.

MORE TO LOVE

There's more to love,
That's what I always say,
Anything to try and make it seem ok.
That my waistline has expanded,
Blowing up like a balloon,
Every time we get that cake and ice-cream,
And I'm reaching for the spoon.
Enough never seems to be enough,
What void am I trying to fill?
Something that's not been fulfilled yet,
By any therapy or pill.

TRIGGER WARNING

Self harm

HARM

There is a voice that tells me,
To cut, to bruise, to hurt,
When I'm feeling too many feelings
And I need that energy to convert,
To something that I can control,
A rhythmic feeling that calms,
I don't do it for attention
Or to cause you any alarm.
Sometimes it is the numbness
That I'm trying to avoid,
Where time has stopped still
And I feel I'm floating in the void.
Pain is a primal reaction,
Our body knows how to react,
When in fact it's our feelings
That are often under attack.
Yes there is a voice that tells me,
To hurt, to cut, to bruise,
And it stops me from giving in,
Because life is what I choose.

It's ok to let others see our sadness. More often than not, they are also looking for a reason to pull their own mask off too.

SHADY SHADES SHELTER SADNESS

Out in the sunlight with a smile on my face,

Fooling everyone with my happiness and knowing my place,

But on the inside I am gasping for air

For the mask on my face hides my true despair.

For shady shades shelter sadness and my sadness likes to hide,

Making it difficult to ever want to confide

Sharing sadness invites judgment, giving it light,

So it's best to keep it hidden and sheltered out of sight.

We must accept that our inner voice isn't always a kind one and we can challenge what it says!

PARANOID MUCH?

Don't get too comfortable,
Don't see success,
Don't believe the worst won't happen,
Don't think you are the best.
No point in being a dreamer,
Dreams rarely do come true,
The world is not your friend my dear,
Everyone is out to get you.

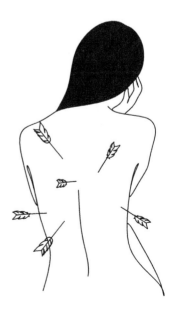

If life was stationary,
it would be pretty boring.

UP/DOWN

Up down go my emotions,

Up down goes my good mood,

Up down goes my waist size,

Depending on my relationship with food.

Up down goes my self belief,

Up down go my reasons to live,

Up down goes my self love,

And the amount of fucks to give.

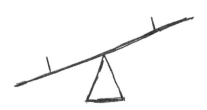

It is ok to set boundaries to avoid burn out. The only one 100% invested in you...is you!

ALL OUT OF STEAM

My energy has dissipated,
After being high for so long,
Trying hard to juggle every plate,
And never to put a foot wrong.
I was a wind-up doll for everyone
And every turn was an expectation,
Clean this, iron that
And never any appreciation.
They kept on winding me up,
To the point of nearly breaking,
Whilst I tried my hardest to give all I had,
With everyone only taking.
My cogs started grinding,
But I had done what was required,
So I'm put on the shelf,
Used, damaged, now retired.

One umbrella isn't going to stop the rain from getting to you, but an army of them can.

BLACK CLOUD

The black cloud is a friend of mine,
It follows me wherever I go,
Looming overhead always,
Whether I'm fast or slow.

History always repeats itself,
That's the lesson it wants me to know,
So that's why it remains my friend even still,
Following me wherever I go.

You can't out run my friend, you see,
It is always two steps ahead,
Even when you're fast asleep,
It can wake you from your bed.

At times it can seem calm and docile,
Nothing but the shadow to bother you,
Then it transforms; grows bigger and stronger,
It's rain of despair soaking you through.

It's futile to think it will ever leave me,
It needs me to keep it strong,
So every once in a while, it lets the sun shine on my face,
But makes sure it's not for too long.

It's always there to remind me,
Of the hurt I have once endured,
To put me back in my place,
If I ever feel self assured.

The flashes it will give me,
As I lie awake at night,
Of every mistake I've ever made
And how I can never seem to make it right.

Make sure to tether yourself to something strong. That way even if you do feel yourself slipping into the void, you'll never drift too far.

THE VOID

The more that I feel that self hate,

The more I reach for the booze and cake,

Trying to fill that empty void,

To ignore those feelings I'm trying to avoid.

Some demons like to be fed,
To make them weaker,
We should starve them instead.

A HOLE GROWS IN MY HEART

A hole grows in my heart,
The cavity knaws away,
At all the belief I had within,
It claims more each passing day.

A hole grows in my heart,
Replacing where hope should be,
Eating away at dreams and desire
Making me question all of me.

A hole grows in my heart,
It spreads just like a cancer,
Turning good to bad, one thought at a time,
Giving me questions, but never the answer.

A hole grows in my heart,
I wish I could cut it out,
For this hole that takes over all of me,
Is one you call self doubt.

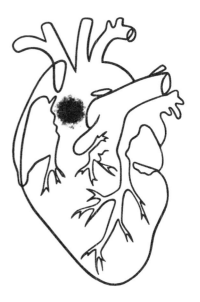

The brighter our own light shines,
the further away the shadows will be.

A SHADOW THAT FOLLOWS

When I venture out,
Or I'm doing something new,
The shadow that I've come to know,
Is always with me too.
It follows me in my car,
It hovers when with my kids,
It reminds me not to get too comfortable,
Complacency it forbids.
It likes me to feel on edge,
A slave to its every whim,
That's when the cramps take hold,
And the nausea then sets in.
The tight feeling in your chest,
Like you barely dare to breathe,
The clamminess of your brow and hands,
As you desperately try to relieve
That feeling like the walls are caving,
And darkness is setting in,
And then your refusal to step outside,
Because you've let your anxiety win.

No ones heart is seamless.
We all have cuts and bruises that we
must take care of.

SEVERAL STITCHES ON MY ONCE SEAMLESS HEART

Life; You don't get out of it alive,
Or unscathed for that matter,
A once seamless heart,
Can so easily tatter.
From a misspent youth,
That once first love of your life,
Who stabbed you once with his manhood,
And the other with a knife.
When he told you, you were the only one for him,
To get you in bed.
But you then realised,
Love was only a word he had said.
Not meant or felt,
And certainly not for you,
That relationship went on to teach
You a lesson or two.
You would be cheated on,
And lied to, betrayed time and again,
And you would try everything in your power
Not to complain.
For your once seamless heart,
Has several stiches now,
From the hurt you have felt,
But recovered from somehow.

Written after the Covid pandemic of 2020, when trying to reconnect with friends seemed so difficult.

SEARCHING

They've all moved on without me,
And I am left behind,
Trying so hard to search through the rubble,
Desperately trying to find,
The part of me that disappeared,
When all the world shut down,
Trying so hard to wear that smile
And mask my hidden frown,
The feelings of deep loneliness,
That makes me feel cold and empty,
Even though we are allowed out in the world,
I still feel caged and not free.
I wish this shadow would pass,
And bring me back to the light,
But I'm like a moth to the flame,
Destroyed by taking flight.

There is such power in writing how we feel and being able to share it with others.

ADULTHOOD

My back hurts,
My life seems a mess,
This adulting thing is hard,
I must confess.
Bringing in a wage,
To pay the bills,
Is not what I thought,
Would give me the thrills,
But stability and consistency
Are words I now use,
With my Tesco click and collect slot,
The main thing I lose.
Clock watching from 2pm
For the dreaded school pick-up,
Refereeing arguments,
Over who has the red cup.
Is this what adulthood is?
Mundane hours of toil,
The only break we get,
Waiting for the kettle to boil?
Though more often than not,
I forget about that too.
Just winging this life thing,
Without any real clue.

My children they look to me,
For guidance and support,
But most of the time I feel,
Like I'm always falling short.
How can I help them,
When I'm the one treading water?
Trying to raise a respectful son
And a strong independent daughter.
Things so uncertain,
Life looking bleak,
Which is why I take up my pen,
In order to speak.
To get it all out there,
To expose frustration and pain,
Anything to stop me
From going insane.

We may not always be happy with what we see in the mirror, but our reflection is only a fraction of what makes us unique.

REFLECTION

When I look into the mirror
I'm not sure who I see.
The person staring back,
No longer feels like me.

She has stopped taking care of herself
Her face is all aflame,
With the redness of embarrassment,
Her deep unhidden shame.

She wanted the world to see,
That everything was not okay,
That all of life's problems,
Were overwhelming each day.

Her actions were a cry for help
For everyone to know,
That she was not coping with life
Despite it looking so.

When she looks into the mirror
There is a stranger staring back
Smiling but dead on the inside,
Finally starting to crack.

It is ok to want to change things about ourselves that are within our area of control. The things outside of that control, we need to find peace with to be happy.

MIRROR MIRROR

Mirror mirror on the wall,
Why couldn't I be thin and tall?
Why couldn't that be tucked up there,
Why couldn't that bit have a little less hair?
Why does that go instantly to my waist?
After what only feels like the smallest taste?
Why does this creak and crack?
Why does that leak?
Why do I find it hard to remember
The words to speak?
Emotions up and down,
Memory like a sieve,
Everyday craving a gin,
With zero fucks to give.

Sometimes the universe keeps giving us lessons, because it is hell bent on ensuring we learn it.

PASSWORD TO UNLOCK THE DOORS OF MY HEART

It should be in a vault, an impenetrable fortress,

But my heart is on display for all to see,

All it needs is a kind word, a compliment,

The time of day, and you have access to all of me.

The doors are revolving, people come and go as they please,

They take what they need and leave little in return,

These abusers are my fatal disease.

But I didn't stop them, I allowed them to take,

They chiselled away at my open heart,

So now I feel the need to build up these doors.

Setting boundaries would be a good start.

I need to encrypt, make it harder to access,

Then I won't be subjected to this pain,

But I never learn, I leave the password on paper,

For you to hurt me all over again.

Believing in fate is believing in a power that we cannot see nor control. We can only do what we can, and hope that our actions lead to the results we wish.

FRAGMENTS OF FATE

The lost ticket, the missed train,
Fated to never see him again?
Is that all that I am, a puppet of fate?
To either show up too early or come too late?
It pulls at my strings and watches me dance,
Making me believe in destiny and the hope of romance,
These fragments of fate or is destiny unwritten?
I refuse to be caged to do destiny's bidding.
Freedom is the punch line of destiny's kidding.

Just because we have been labelled something, doesn't mean we can't take a sharpie and do some editing.

BAGGAGE

I pick up each bag I own
And take a look at each label,
Each word written there
Is one that will enable
Me to never make a change,
For I carry them and hold them tight,
Not even thinking for one second
If any of these labels are actually right.
This one says I'm too fat,
That other one says I'm a failure
And every time I take a bite out of life,
The moments each taste staler.
I'm not good enough, I'll never amount
To what people thought I could be,
I'm not ambitious enough, then I'm too obsessed,
It feels exhausting being me.
I wish I could throw away these bags,
Or let them burn away,
Letting each flame take the feelings,
I've allowed too long to stay.
The weight has become so familiar,
Who would I be without them there?
Just a girl; simple and unburdened,
Finally letting go of her despair.

Everyone will see a different side to your story, this is why it's so important to speak out about how you are feeling so people know yours.

VIEWPOINT

The child

I just want to play with her,

Why does she not love me?

I want to tell her about my day,

And share with her my glee

I tell her I am hungry

She snaps at me and says,

"Just wait another minute will you",

She says that every day.

I want to get her attention,

So I do something she can't ignore,

Like hurting my little sister

Or spilling my drink all over the floor.

I just want her to see me,

To be the mommy I had before,

But she never wants to be with me,

She prefers to work more and more.

She never smiles like she used to,

I catch her crying in her room,

I just want to feel close to her,

Her baby that once was in the womb.

But now I just turn away from her,

It hurts too much to try,

Now it's not just her anymore

That hides away to cry.

Husband

I try and be all romantic,

I'm definitely in the mood,

I've served her, her favourite wine,

And made her, her favourite food.

I try and be suggestive,

A playful touch here and there,

She recoils at my touch,

And stares out into thin air.

I try to make some plans,

For something we both can do,

She looks at me bewildered,

She doesn't have a clue.

She can't pick a single thing,

She can't make any decision,

She never remembers the things I say,

She needs constant supervision.

Otherwise she wouldn't feed herself,

Nor drink a single glass.

If I knew this was what marriage would be

I may have taken a pass.

Friend

This is the third time I've tried to arrange
To see my best friend this week,
I try and ask her about what's going on
But I can tell she doesn't want to speak.
She is only good at cancelling,
Messaging me at the very last hour,
I'm sick to death of rearranging my life
Around this flaky, delicate flower.
Does my time mean nothing?
Am I not important too?
I don't think she thinks that far ahead,
Or thinks any decision through.
Why say yes if you're not going to come?
Just save me the headache next time,
I want to go out and live my life,
Whilst I am still in my prime!

Teacher

She's always late for drop offs,
She finds it difficult to connect,
When I'm trying to tell her about his day,
When she has finally come to collect.
I've got some real concerns,
For their family life at home,
She seems fixated on work,
And is always glued to her phone.
Her son he craves her attention,
She doesn't seem able to give it,
There seems to be something deeper going on,
As she never seems fully with it.
I will do my due diligence just to ensure,
The boy knows he is safe and protected,
From whatever troubles are happening at home,
That make him feel sad and rejected.

The wife

I couldn't hate myself more,
Than I do in this very moment,
Standing there across the boxing ring
Is my next undefeated opponent.

The person I am fighting knows too much,
They know my every move,
Every blow I try to land on them,
Is pointless, I can't improve.

This person wears my face,
My body mirrors theirs,
And every time I look in their eyes
She only returns the stares.

The child was only asking for food,
She gives him a curt reply,
He leaves the room empty handed,
And forces out a regretful sigh.

The man tried to show me love,
She swats his hand away
I keep wondering what will break his hope,
The hope that makes him stay.

I scream at her to stop it,
It's my life she is destroying,
And all the people's emotions,
She has such pleasure in toying.

The friend tries to hold out her hand,
And begs me to take it quick,
But she is already there,
With a punch that makes me sick.

I'm all alone and isolated,
With only her voice inside my head,
Telling me I am fat and ugly,
How it would be better if I were dead.

One day I may take her up on that
When the pain of fighting becomes too much,
But for now I'll keep on fighting,
Till the day I feel happiness's touch.

What we surround ourselves with is of the upmost importance in creating a happy life. If we are surrounded by chaos and negativity, we start to feel like our life is chaotic and negative.

CLUTTER

Life crumbles apart around me,
Through unticked to-do lists,
Washing and ironing pile stacking up,
And bundles of unwanted bits.
So what do I do to combat it?
What is the solution I need to find?
To not only unclutter my surroundings,
But to also unclutter my mind?
I still don't have the answer,
Life is teaching me bit by bit,
How to handle what it throws at me,
And make lemonade out of lemons with it.

If only we saw the light in ourselves that others see in us.

CRYSTALLISED REFLECTIONS

Thick black eyeliner, black dyed hair,

Listening to sad songs that reflected her despair.

Grunting and shouting, felt so misunderstood,

Going through this patch of life where she never felt truly good.

Fast forward a bit, now she is blonde and girly,

Using straighteners at times though mainly keeping curly.

She lives life in colour, trying to stand out from the crowd,

Many see her as confident, funny, loud and proud.

Inside her heart is breaking for the reflection that she sees,

Is one she is never happy with, she thinks it will never please.

Now she is a mother, she finally settled down,

But although she is Queen at home, she doesn't wear a crown.

The reflection may have changed; the hair, the fads and clothes,

But one thing that remained the same was the sadness in her eyes that grows,

This crystallised reflection of a girl who doesn't see,

That despite the sadness she carries, she is a light for you and me.

Journaling in the moment, is a wonderful way of keeping the memories alive as they happen. Not allowing time to mould them into something they aren't.

THROUGH THE TUNNEL OF TIME

Smiles stare back at me
Are any of them real?
I try to recall each moment
A party, night out or meal.

These pictures capture a moment,
A moment frozen in time,
Though every moment through these photos,
No longer feel like mine.

I wish I could go back
To the moment captured within,
But then I remember even then,
I wasn't comfortable in my own skin,
Wishing to be prettier, taller, smarter and thin.

This tunnel of time ensnares me,
It keeps me looking back,
Haunted by my past failings,
Feels like the present is under attack.

Memories can be distorted,
Altered by our perception,
Our brain is oh so clever,
And does this for our protection.

To shield us from difficulties,
Or exonerate us from blame,
To remind us of our trauma
So we can avoid more of the same.

The tunnel of time can be a blessing,
But it can also be a curse,
So it's important that we focus,
On not making our situation worse.
Don't look back with regret,
On the things you didn't achieve,
But find comfort in all the joy and love,
In your life you did receive.

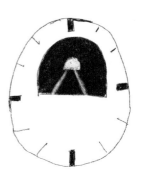

Having feeling like I had been asleep for the best part of a couple of years; drifting through life. I now feel back in control and ready to take on the world...starting with this book!

AWAKE

With eyes that were firmly shut,
I shuffled throughout the day,
Ignoring what was in my gut
The things I should do or say.

I was fast asleep and dreaming,
Hoping life would be over soon,
Whilst dreaming of those who were seeming
To avoid disasters as if immune.

I stopped looking in the mirror,
Afraid of what I may see,
But the need to change became clearer
With my body aches and growing misery.

Life around me had fallen apart,
But my blinkered vision wouldn't allow
Me to see the destruction or to start
To work out how to fix the here and now.

I needed a gun to my head,
An excessive wake up call,
Otherwise I'd be better off dead
As this wasn't living at all.

Consumed by external pressure
I was about to spontaneously combust,
A new year and I'm feeling fresher,
I just needed some time to adjust.

To see the beauty right in front of me,
To open up my eyes
To no longer be an absentee
But instead hear my battle cries.

We so often feel that we have to be everything to everyone so much, that we don't have anything left in the tank for ourselves. It's ok to be selfish sometimes.

TOUGH ACT TO FOLLOW

Today I don't have the energy,
To be that funny guy,
And I know as soon as the wisecracks stop,
They will be asking why.
I've set with them a precedence,
That entertainment is all that I am,
That other's happiness goes above my own,
As that has always been my plan.
I love making people happy,
Love putting a smile on a face,
Knowing that I have achieved this,
Makes me feel like I've found my place.
I feel connected to those around me,
Knowing that I have touched their lives,
Then waiting for that moment,
When my own happiness arrives.
But happiness can be fleeting,
If we are constantly waiting for our chance,
We should take happiness in each moment,
Learn the rhythm of its dance.
If people cannot truly accept me,
For each different side I possess,
Then they never really cared for me,
And all the feelings I wish to express.
I can't always be Mrs Funny,
Mrs jazz hands and jokes galore,
And I need to learn to accept this,
Because who am I doing it for?

There's nothing better than the feeling of hope that things can and will get better.

RECHARGE YE OLD BATTERIES

When I lie awake and ponder of the things I have to do,
I often feel overwhelmed, thinking every step through.
The to-do list never gets shorter, it's added to every day,
So I procrastinate and hide, anything to delay
The inevitability of fulfilling, the ever growing list,
Not feeling like I'm living, but just made to exist.
I can't pretend anymore that everything's alright,
I can't get all of my feelings and hide them out of sight.
So sometimes I need to give in to my desire to be alone,
To re-energise and recuperate, to feel back in the zone.
The zone where I'm thriving, and not always on my guard,
Living my life with my batteries finally fully charged.

'This too shall pass' may sound cliché,
but learning to reframe negative thoughts,
creates a happier and healthier today.

PHOENIX RISING

PHOENIX RISING

Though there has been times of real strife, there have also been fantastic moments of renewal, rejuvenation and the birth of phrases like 'living your best life', 'lit', 'YOLO' and 'next level'.

These are poems that all reflect the feeling of being uplifted. Feeling like we are 'nailing it' at life and also where we have seen darker days but come out the other side feeling stronger. If you need a pick me up this is the chapter for you!

It would have been easier to just have a book that was all about good vibes, but toxic positivity can be just as damaging as negativity. Its ok to validate your feelings of sadness; life isn't always on an upward trajectory. Sometimes we hit bumps along the way and what we have to remember is once we've hit rock bottom, the only way is up!

Once you have come through the other side of mental health struggles it will always be something that you have to work on, just like with physical health. If you start to let things slip then there is a good chance you could relapse, that's why it's really important to have a toolkit for your mental health; tips and tricks that you know have helped you overcome hurdles before. Things like picking up this book and being reminded that you are not alone in your struggle and that you can and will find a way to get through this. Things like going for a walk, listening to your favourite song or watching your favourite movie. Journaling, reaching out to a friend or family member, reaching out to a professional. Have a toolkit that you can refer back to, to help you feel healthy in body and mind.

Throughout this chapter you will also be subjected to life's many positive affirmations, at the end of this book there will be activities to help you on your journey to better mental health, including how to use affirmations and how to create your own.

Included are a selection of the poems that are a part of my magnetic mantra gift sets. These feature 10 random mini poems on business card sized magnets. The idea is to use it as a game to pick an envelope at random in the hope that the card you pick is the one you need to hear that day. Each card comes in its own envelope so you can also choose to gift them to someone else that may need a pick me up! To find out more head over to my website www.athenasbounty.co.uk and check out the poetry products collection.

CHANGE THE RHETORIC

Is it really that bad to put myself first?
If I did that once in a while, what is the worst
That could happen to those around me?
Would they have the eyes to see
That I sometimes need that time to just simply be?
We always put our needs to the bottom of the pile,
So we can nurture everyone else whilst plastering on the smile.
Our thoughts and feelings don't matter,
All us women are good for is chatter,
But I refuse to play that part,
Cause when I speak, I speak from the heart.
We have moved on from not being heard,
Where our voices were muted even in the written word,
It's not selfish to want to be more,
Than a mother or a wife, doing chores.

Self care can mean so many things,
Independence and all that it brings,
Pampering, meditation and art,
Going to bed early to get a good start,
Feeling empowered and uplifting others,
Supporting other business mothers,
Put yourself first, do what you love,
Someone takes the low road; you just rise above.
They will tell you there's more important things,
But it's only with self-love that you can grow wings;
To fly above the negativity that bites and stings.
So is it really bad to put yourself first?
No, change the rhetoric we've been versed.

I am worthy

❀ — ❀ — ❀ — ❀ — ❀

It is enough just to be myself,
And in accepting that,
is where I find my wealth.

❀ — ❀ — ❀ — ❀ — ❀

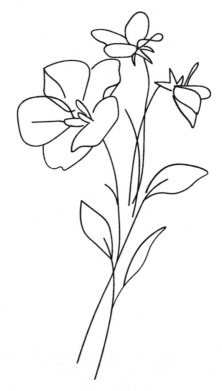

I am loved

OPEN YOUR EYES 2.0

Open your eyes,
What do you see?
An incomplete picture,
Showing me.
My destiny unwritten
What will I achieve?
I can do anything,
If I just believe.

I am strong

❀ — ❀ — ❀ — ❀ — ❀

A brand new day to unfold,
So don't wait around for change,
Be bold!

❀ — ❀ — ❀ — ❀ — ❀

I am enough

DISCOVERY

I've finally found the balance,
I finally feel in touch,
I don't feel like I'm doing too little,
And I don't feel like it's all too much.
The plates are still all spinning,
I've put some broken ones back together,
They feel more strong and sturdy now,
They won't fall from the weight of a feather.
I feel a certain sense of calm,
That I am now on the right track,
And I need to keep going forward,
To stop always needing to look back.
For back is not where I'll find my answers,
They are out there yet to be uncovered,
My full potential, the best version of me,
Is about to be discovered.

I am a gift

❀ — ❀ — ❀ — ❀ — ❀

New beginning,
Time for winning,
My negativity is thinning,
Time for change,
To be on the right page,
For the world is my musical
And I am on the stage.

❀ — ❀ — ❀ — ❀ — ❀

I am full of wonder

FRAGILE

I'm as fragile as a grain of sand,
Fired up and turned to glass,
I'm as fragile as a spider's web,
Or a single blade of grass.
I'm as fragile as carbon dust,
Tiny specks you can barely see,
But if you apply enough pressure,
You can make a diamond out of me.

I am Strong

❀ — ❀ — ❀ — ❀ — ❀

I am enough, I am loved,
I am a gift from above,
And sometimes we need reminding,
Of that strength we feel is hiding,
Look within and you will see,
You are everything you need to be!

❀ — ❀ — ❀ — ❀ — ❀

I believe in myself

YOUR WHY

When the sales are running dry and engagement is low,
Reminding myself of why I started is where I go.
To think back to a time where I felt so lost,
Makes me strive for success, but at what cost?
Sometimes my mental health suffers from my demands,
As my ever growing to-do list, beckons more commands.
It's important to remember why, but to never go too far,
Because if you do that, you can start to forget, who you really are.

My power is unlimited

❀ — ❀ — ❀ — ❀ — ❀

A fire burns within you,
It shows you where passions lie,
If you pursue what you love to do,
You won't just walk, you'll fly.

❀ — ❀ — ❀ — ❀ — ❀

With every challenge I face,
its with ease

BRAVE

Feel the fear and do it anyway
Is the definition of being brave,
It's not giving in to all those temptations,
That surround us and make us crave.
What you can unlock inside of you
Is so much more than you even knew you could,
It's time to start believing in yourself,
To begin to feel truly good.
So push past those feelings of self doubt,
Of fear of not fulfilling your goal,
The power of your destiny is within you,
Your success is all in your control.

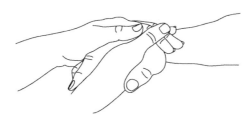

I see the beauty in everything

❀ — ❀ — ❀ — ❀ — ❀

True healing can only begin
When we learn to love ourselves
from within.

❀ — ❀ — ❀ — ❀ — ❀

My life is full of magic and serendipity

YOU ARE A GIFT

Hello today, goodbye tomorrow,
Gone are the tears I've cried,
Gone is the sorrow
I stand strong for all to see
That it is enough just being me.
Yesterday's pain was yesterday's lesson,
That we should count each day as if it's a blessing,
Know deep inside that you have the strength,
To fight every fight with every breath.
You are amazing just look at you go,
Believe those kind words that are telling you so.
You are loved so much, don't forget that is true,
You are loved by simply being YOU!

Everyone sees how much love I have

inside

Confidence is learnt
Respect is earnt
Perserverance is proven,
Failure makes us human.

I choose to do great things today

THREAD BY THREAD

Thread by thread,
Seam by seam,
Not knowing what to do,
Or what it might mean
Caged like an animal,
Waiting for release,
Prodded and poked
Without a moment of peace.
Praying for the end of this,
With some hope in sight
Letting go of this darkness
And stepping into the light.

I am thankful for today

❀ — ❀ — ❀ — ❀ — ❀

Breathe in, breathe out,
Let only positivity shout,
Let it drown out all the hate,
That has become too easy to create.

❀ — ❀ — ❀ — ❀ — ❀

I am in control of my thoughts

MY HEART IN YOUR HANDS

I smile at you from across the room,
And your smile reaches your eyes,
We spoke for hours about the folly of life,
Your attention took me by surprise.
You listened to every word I said,
And laughed at every joke,
You offered to buy me something stronger,
I was happy with my diet coke.
Eating, drinking wasn't important,
They were all distractions from you,
But my inner saboteur couldn't help themselves,
They needed to know if your interest was true.
So she delved deep into the box of trauma,
Picking out the best juicy morsel to share,
I was going to put my heart in your hands,
And see how much you would care.

Would you take what you heard and caress me,
Promise you would never do that to me?
Or would you judge me to be damaged goods,
Too much work a guarantee?
I see you sit and ponder,
Taking all that I say in,
Then you take my hands in yours,
And tell me my real adventure is yet to begin.

I don't need outside validation.
I don't need to be made up or thin,
I just need to start showing love,
To the beauty that lies within.
My past doesn't need to define me,
My scars are no ones business but my own,
And that until I started to realise this,
I would always end up alone.
He got up and kissed my forehead,
And I knew that he was THE one,
But I needed time to figure me out,
To be the woman I'm meant to become.

I love myself and I allow others
to love me too

❀ — ❀ — ❀ — ❀ — ❀

You are powerful and strong,
Determined and capable.
Just look at you go,
You will be unstoppable!

❀ — ❀ — ❀ — ❀ — ❀

I am proud of myself because
I know I am doing my best

JUST KEEP SWIMMING

Oxygen running low. No where to go,

Swimming in the caves taking every corner slow.

There it is, air at last,

I lift my head, to take a blast,

Hoping for air, but more water there,

Wondering how long, my oxygen tank will fare.

The light at the end of the dark cave, I need it to guide me home,

I need to feel the fresh air in my lungs, and have the freedom to roam.

I took a risk, and now I'm stuck,

I hope I find my way out, I will with any luck

Yet still the cave goes on, and the light grows dimmer by the day,

And although it seems futile, my hope will guide the way.

I take joy in every small step I make

✽ — ✽ — ✽ — ✽ — ✽

Sometimes the path is winding,
Our choices overwhelmingly blinding,
But you need to have faith to view,
The power that lives within you.

✽ — ✽ — ✽ — ✽ — ✽

I'm happy that I'm healthy,
powerful and unique

SOMETIMES

Sometimes I ache inside, sometimes I'm numb
Sometimes that darkness within me, feels like it's won
Sometimes I'm angry, sometimes I'm mean,
Sometimes I shout, just to feel like I'm seen.
Sometimes I like me, sometimes I don't
How can I expect others to like me, when I won't?

Sometimes I feel empty, sometimes I feel full
Sometimes that darkness within me has a stronger pull
Sometimes I feel strong, sometimes I feel weak
Sometimes I don't have the energy to even speak
Sometimes I cry, and sometimes I laugh
But no matter how I feel, I will find the right path.

I'm proud of what I've
accomplished so far

❀ — ❀ — ❀ — ❀ — ❀

If at first you don't succeed,
In achieving all your plans
Do not fear, all will be right,
Your destiny is within your hands.

❀ — ❀ — ❀ — ❀ — ❀

I enjoy the present moment
and cherish my existence

OPEN YOUR WINGS

Open your wings
And take a deep breath,
Never feel
That you are out of your depth.
It is in doing what scares us,
That we learn and we grow,
So don't hold on to your fears,
Just let them all go.

I am in the process of positive change

❀ — ❀ — ❀ — ❀ — ❀

The whole world's a stage,
I'm ready to present,
A brand new character,
Who is strong and confident.

❀ — ❀ — ❀ — ❀ — ❀

I am strong in the belief
that I can succeed

MINDSET SHIFT

We are all the creation of miracles,
We are all created unique,
And our harshest critic is within us,
And we need to teach it to speak,
With kindness and love and understanding,
And not just for everyone else,
We need to turn some of that love around,
And give it more to ourself.

I am always focused and determined

❀ — ❀ — ❀ — ❀ — ❀

Flowers bloom and die,
Beauty fades as well,
But a beautiful soul, just like yours,
Has everyone forever under its spell.

❀ — ❀ — ❀ — ❀ — ❀

I am perfect just the way I am

A WOMAN'S JUGGLE

We are bold, we are courageous,

Our passion and strength contagious,

Just look at us and see,

How we fought so hard to be free.

Free from gender discrimination,

Free from masculine dictation,

Free to show the world what we're all about,

Free to be heard with talk not a shout.

We are workers, we are the Queen,

Yet we still struggle to be seen,

Seen as more than just a mother,

Or as a man's significant other.

We love fiercely and we fight the same,

Competing in a man's game,

We will succeed, do more than breed,

Because our strength is what's in need.

I can make my dreams come true

❀ — ❀ — ❀ — ❀ — ❀

The rain can keep on pouring,
Because I know for sure,
Rainbows and clear skies,
Are what's next in store.

❀ — ❀ — ❀ — ❀ — ❀

I am brave

TURN THAT FROWN UPSIDE DOWN

When life is getting on top of you,

And you don't know what's up and what's down,

You can always try and make a smile,

From what was once a frown.

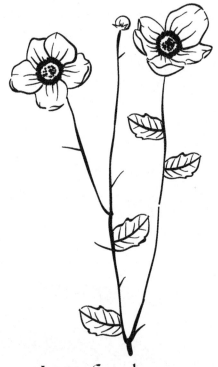

I am fearless

❀ — ❀ — ❀ — ❀ — ❀

Love the life you live,
Take that love and give,
Share it all around,
In the places it can't be found

❀ — ❀ — ❀ — ❀ — ❀

I am bold

A HANDFUL OF HOPE

Sometimes the path seems endless,
Shrouded in darkness and pain,
Sometimes things start to unravel,
Overwhelm pours down on you like rain.

It can feel so empty and lonely,
Like you are on an island stranded.
Every time you get close to escaping
The area already expanded.

But then there is something that can dispel this,
The light that comes shining through,
The relief that this is not forever,
That there is hope for you.

A handful of hope is all you need,
It can spread fast like a wild fire,
So put together your negative thoughts,
And burn them on the funeral pyre.

I am courageous

Showered, dressed
And ready to impress!

I am successful and confident

LITTLE VOICE

That little voice keeps talking to you,
Telling you that you're no good,
You'll never amount to this or that,
You'll never be all you could
But tell that voice to pipe on down,
It doesn't know your destination,
It raises its damn ugly head
Without a moments hesitation,
You tell it, you know where you are going,
And that it's only talking out of fear,
Because you know who you really are,
And you are stronger than you might appear.

I can let go of
what doesn't serve me

❀ — ❀ — ❀ — ❀ — ❀

Be wild and free,

Happiness is key!

❀ — ❀ — ❀ — ❀ — ❀

I am confident

BEGINNING OF ANOTHER END

I thought that life had purpose,
But death has purpose too,
For it reminds us that there is no permanence,
In anything we say or do.
A wrong can soon be righted,
With a last breath, comes a new-born cry,
Every up, becomes a down,
And every hello, becomes a goodbye.

Life ends, so life can love,
Borrowed energy being returned,
Just like a phoenix rising from the ashes,
Once its old body has tragically burned.
It is the beginning of another end,
When another door unlocks,
And will you go through the open door,
When it's destiny that knocks?

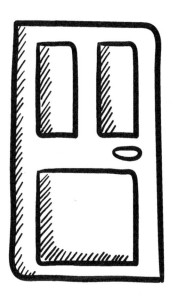

I am a marvel to behold

❀ — ❀ — ❀ — ❀ — ❀

Love lets us ride on feathers
Swirling up and around the air
It sparks in us imagination
To think of ways to show we care.

❀ — ❀ — ❀ — ❀ — ❀

I can achieve anything
I put my mind to

I AM IMPORTANT

I am important, why can't he see?
That doing these things, is what I do for me.
It makes me feel alive, it brings me contentment,
When all I seem to feel from him is his resentment
Why can't he believe in me? See my determination?
All I ever sense from him is his growing frustration
Money and happiness are not made in the same way,
Seeking one can lead to fulfilment, the other to decay.
I am whole in this home I've made, with my poetry to guide me,
Loving living in the moment that's made with my creativity.

I am balanced

❀ — ❀ — ❀ — ❀ — ❀

Hello again that dark I've known
I knew you couldn't leave me alone,
But even though you are still here,
Positive thoughts can make you
disappear.

❀ — ❀ — ❀ — ❀ — ❀

I can establish boundaries

that I can maintain

YOU ARE SPECIAL

There is only one of you,
You know that is true,
And because of this
You are special.

Your beauty and grace,
The smile on your face
And because of this
You are special.

Your courage and wisdom
The queen of the kingdom
And because of this
You are special.

In all that you do,
Making old, feel like new,
You are special to me,
Like I am special to you.

I can trust that every hardship

is a lesson I needed

❀ — ❀ — ❀ — ❀ — ❀

Flowers that bloom the fastest,
Often have nowhere further to go,
So don't rush the beautiful process,
To find the right place to grow.

❀ — ❀ — ❀ — ❀ — ❀

I am worthy of happiness

SOLITARY

One; a singular person
Not shackled to expectations
Of others, free to live life in exultation
Under covers. No burden, no pain, no grief,
No disappointment, reliance or disbelief.
Just living a life of solitary refinement,
Until I can find those who I am in alignment.

I attract only good things into my life

❀ — ❀ — ❀ — ❀ — ❀

When you're not content with the image,

That you see when you look in the mirror,

Sometimes it helps to change perspective,

To see your inner beauty more clearer.

❀ — ❀ — ❀ — ❀ — ❀

I can look for creative solutions
to any problem I encounter

BOSS LADY

I am the boss lady,
What I say goes,
I feel large and in charge,
From my head to my toes.
The world tries to control me,
Tries to keep me in line,
But I'm not one to be tamed,
Any decision I make, will be mine.

I am surrounded

by love and kindness

❀ — ❀ — ❀ — ❀ — ❀

We all learn and we grow,
And all at our own pace,
So don't try and compete with those
around you,
Your life doesn't have to be a rat race.

❀ — ❀ — ❀ — ❀ — ❀

I am unique

THE CRACK

A tiny crack, that's all it needs,

And there from my insecurities and fears it feeds.

The gap it widens, letting more shit in,

The feeling of overwhelm, not knowing where to begin.

I try to remember to have courage and faith,

To go into that happy place that makes me feel safe,

Sometimes it's ok to scream, cry and shout,

It's the only way that overspill of emotion can get out.

Confide in your partner, a relative or friend,

It's only in sharing, that we don't have to pretend.

That everything is perfect, to paint over that crack,

To know that someone else understands and has your back.

Let's seal up that crack with love and kindness

Focus on what is to come instead of the trauma behind us.

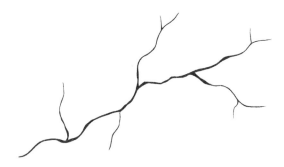

I am important

❀ — ❀ — ❀ — ❀ — ❀

So many invisible illnesses,
So many hidden scars,
Have patience and love for each other,
Picture each person like a bright
shining star.

❀ — ❀ — ❀ — ❀ — ❀

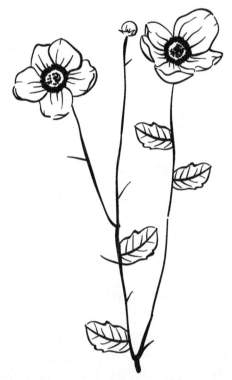

I forgive myself for not being perfect

EMPOWERED

Hello world, this is me,
When you look at my face,
What do you see?
Someone timid and shy?
Or confident and sassy?
Someone down to earth
Or posh and classy?
Someone all put together
Or falling apart?
Someone open with no filter
Or keeps cards
Close to their heart?
No matter what you see,
No matter what you perceive
See empowerment,
That's what I want you to believe.

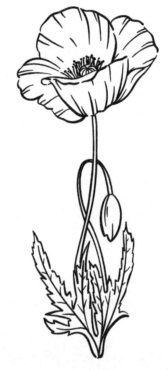

I deserve to have
happy relationships

❀ — ❀ — ❀ — ❀ — ❀

Kindness costs nothing,
So we can give it without a price,
And when we share our compassion
with others,
It helps to break the ice,
To those who may be struggling,
with their day to day life.

❀ — ❀ — ❀ — ❀ — ❀

I am ready to accept

and receive miracles

BELIEVE AND RECEIVE

Today is the day that I believe in me,
For I want that freedom to truly be,
Happy with all that I am and all that I do,
And spreading that happiness to others too.
When life feels overwhelming as it often can,
I know that every action is part of a greater plan.
Life often works in mysterious ways,
Where mistakes are made but the lesson stays,
The lesson to keep going, that you can make it through,
Because to your family and friends you are the glue.

Children should come with an
instruction manual, and with an off
button

BLOOD, S*** AND TEARS

BLOOD, S*** AND TEARS

Motherhood has always been portrayed as this beautiful journey, and don't get me wrong it can be beautiful. It can give you all the sunshine and rainbow moments you've ever dreamed of, but it can also make you feel lonely, isolated, a shadow of your former self, lost, out of control, overwhelmed and depressed.

This is the camp that I was in. I loved my children but I also felt suffocated by motherhood. I lost who I was and felt so out of my depth I was drowning in breast pumps, sleep schedules and trying to balance cleaning, laundry, work and basic hygiene.

I was diagnosed with Post-Natal depression and began the process of coming to terms with the fact that I hated being out of control of my own life. What started it all off was having OC (obstetric cholestasis) through both my pregnancies, which meant on both occasions I couldn't have the birth I wanted and was forced to be induced early. Now I know to most that may not seem like a bad thing, but with my daughter that meant having to give birth without the support of my family who were away, and that made a huge difference to my birthing experience. This is the time where I make the first of my thank yous to the wonderful staff at Home-Start North-East Worcestershire for their support during this difficult time. They offered me courses, referred me to therapies, offered a safe space and a listening ear. The work they do to support families in need is incredible.

Whenever we go on social media we have motherhood, and more importantly how to be the perfect mother shoved in our faces. This is what we should be feeding our children, this is how we should discipline. They "should" have organic, hand carved out of wood toys, we should be taking them to XYZ for Halloween, Christmas etc for the sake of the Instagram grid. Is it any wonder that most of us don't feel like we are doing a good job? Back in my folk's days they didn't see what Jane down the road was up to in her spare time, but although social media has the power to connect, it also has the power to isolate us too; with us constantly comparing ourselves to our peers every step of the way.

So this chapter is for the moms out there that don't feel like they are bossing it. This is your reminder that you are not alone in this and that you also have totally got this! It takes a village to raise a child...make sure your asking for help when you need it and talking to the right people when you are struggling (and by the right people, I mean those who aren't going to judge you, and those you aren't feeling threatened by with those insecurities of yours). As this chapter takes you through the many milestones our children go through, I hope it helps you find some peace and helps you to laugh a little too.

WAITING ROOM THOUGHTS

Anxiously waiting for your imminent arrival,

Your reliance on me key to your survival,

You will be so small, but it's me who feels small,

Overwhelmed by the sheer weight of it all.

You'll be in my arms and I won't be able to pretend,

How motherhood will change me in ways I can't comprehend.

I'm scared, can I admit that? When one becomes two,

When you are pushed from my womb to make your grand

debut.

Can I do this? Of course I can,

For my heart saw and loved you when your heartbeat began.

Push, rip, gasp, cry,
A crescendo of life,
Followed by a lullaby.

OXYTOCIN

The pain grips me intently,
As the Oxytocin does its job,
The contractions coming thick and fast,
Makes me practically sob.

I go into a safe space,
Deep within my head,
And imagine I am anywhere else,
But in this hospital bed.

The midwife checks for dilation,
It's not yet time to push,
I still can't believe I'm letting a stranger,
Anywhere near my bush.

The urge gets ever greater,
And I don't care what she says,
I need to get this baby out,
But my head is in a haze.

They think I need something stronger,
But I know I can withhold,
Just give me the damn gas and air,
Entonox; a pure gassy breath of gold.

I feel it in, well...I'm not sure where,
That now is really the time,
She double checks; 10 cm,
And my cervix is in its prime.

I can't quite explain the sensation,
It's like having a really large poo,
Except you're not alone, but surrounded,
And your other half is watching too.

There's nothing dignified about this experience,
As you finally emerge from within,
Shot out from my vagina like a canon,
Putting the midwives' heads in a spin.

But I've done it, it's finally over,
And I push back my sweat soaked hair,
When they hand me my beautiful baby,
Then inform me I've unfortunately had a tear.

When you become a parent you realise how many words are created to explain some situations you would never normally imagine yourself in.

This poem relates to words such as Poonami: A wave of poo that consumes all in its path. Poomagedon/poopagedon, poosplosion, apoocalyse, shituation and shitastrophy just to name a few.

POOMAGEDON

The day had seemed so perfect,
We snuggled and cuddled at home,
But how was I to know that something,
Was going to so abruptly lower the tone?

I'd put you in your car seat,
To go for a meet up in town,
All the while not realising,
You were brewing something soft
and greeny-brown.

I met with the other mothers,
We were swapping birthing stories and sipping
tea,
You started squirming and crying you wanted
out,
And soon from your car seat you were free.

But oh my gosh,
A smell erupts,
And from my conversation,
It interrupts.

Not just any poo,
But a Poomagedon,
Up your back and down your legs,
I feel my face redden.

The café toilet not equipped,
For the sheer colossal amount of shit,
I admit, I had not prepared,
How I was to deal with it.

The other moms showed such support,
But from my meet up I had to abort,
For no amount of wet wipes,
Were going to do the trick,
From your poonami explosion,
Which nearly made me sick.

And although for me it was a trauma,
For you it was just another day,
And at least it was contained to your car seat,
And not all over the bloomin' softplay!

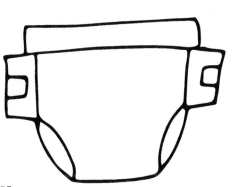

Who knew so many of us would choose a path that leads to an actual form of torture...sleep deprivation.

ZZZZZZZ

My eyes are getting heavy,
They're begging me to close,
But when you have a baby,
That's not how the story goes.

Because right when you get comfortable,
When a content sigh escapes your lips,
It's that time to go to the nursery,
For one of your many nightly trips.

It could be their tummy rumbling for milk,
Or maybe they've lost their dummy,
Perhaps they've got an appendage stuck,
Or they just want a cuddle from mommy.

Whatever the reason may be
For the 3am party at home,
You'll have opportunities to learn new lullabies,
Or trying white-noise apps on your phone.

You'll find you need matchsticks to keep eyes
open,
And you'll often fall asleep on the job,
That's when your baby will lovingly scream,
Or hit you square in the gob.

Because their purpose for being so loud,
Is to make sure that you stay awake,
Even though you may be longing for bed
And sleep the commodity you forsake.

You are their whole wide world now,
And when you're gone, they don't understand,
That you're only in the next room,
They think they're abandoned and left unmanned.

That's why that piercing cry,
The one that seems so melodramatic,
Means so much more to them,
For your loss to them is traumatic.

But when they see your weary face,
They know they're not alone,
For within your arms, they are safe from harm,
From everything to them, unknown.

So whilst this sleep deprivation
Is making you a cranky mother,
Remember how much your baby loves you,
For them, there is no other.

And I know it's not much consolation,
As you sob it's 3 in the morning,
But every baby book you'd have ever read,
Did give you plenty of warning.

And lack of sleep is no easy feat,
When you're expected to function like before,
So take the time out when you can,
To sail away on sleep's waves and restore.

I remember being so excited about starting weaning...and then, I started. It's funny how quickly excitement can be replaced.

I LOVE WEARING CARROTS

I had never been so excited,
For this brand new experience to unfold,
I had bought all the ingredients I would need,
And listened to all advice I'd been told,

Weaning; something different from milk,
I just couldn't wait for you to try,
What I didn't expect is your lack of interest,
Or indeed how far food could fly.

You smushed it all up in your hands,
But nothing ever made it to lips,
I took again, to all my books,
Trying to learn some tips.

My homemade veg and pureed fruit,
Just didn't hit your brief,
But give you an Ella's kitchen pouch,
And to my absolute disbelief,
You lapped it up,
You demanded more,
So despite the costs,
I raced back to the store.
Desperate for you to eat food,
That wouldn't end up on the floor.

And as you grew,
You tried new things,
But not anything I'd cooked,
Which I won't lie, still stings.

Preferring pre-made,
And bought from a shop,
I'm still desperately trying,
To make the swap.

To healthy eating,
Foods that aren't beige,
Putting broccoli and carrots on your plate,
And hoping you'll engage.

But you like what you like,
And you're as stubborn as they come,
So enjoy what you're eating,
And maybe one day you'll succumb.

So much of our motherhood journey is following advice from others more knowledgeable than us. But, we have to remember that we can still make our own choices about how best to parent OUR children. Remember we know our children, better than anyone. Happy mum, happy baby.

BREAST IS BEST

I remember a time,
Where breasts were on my mind,
And I felt totally undermined,
About my nipples perked and primed.
For these lumps of tissue that adorned my body,
That once made me feel sexy,
Were now a feeding apparatus for a new-born,
Which I found altogether quite perplexing.
They nuzzled and they screamed,
When they needed another feed,
Every half an hour for milk
You'd once again start to plead.
I found it really difficult,
To get the latch just right,
And each time you slipped off the breast,
You'd have a rather nasty fright.
I learnt a lot about let down
As my milk shot out like a water gun,
But unlike a typical water gun fight,
Milk everywhere was nowhere near as fun.
Tongue tie became a word,
That frequented many conversations,
As nipples cracked and bled,
Leading to pain and added frustrations.
All demonstrations led to my reservations,
That I would never get the hang of these feeding operations,
But my obligation to stick at,
Something that caused me so much aggravation,
Led me to the conclusion,
That I could change my situation.

I decided to take back control
Of the body I once owned
And started to use a bottle,
Which no midwife would condone.
But you know what, I felt freer,
I began to enjoy my journey
As your mother and protector,
I began to feel more worthy.
For I had pushed aside all the rhetoric,
Of what others said I should do,
And looked deep within my own heart,
At the path I wished to pursue.
Breast is best, may be true,
But really at what cost?
When you're forcing it on a mother,
Who already feels like her battle is lost.

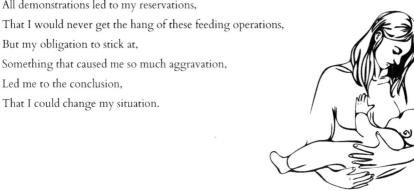

Why do we find it so difficult as mothers to give ourselves credit?

We birthed and keep alive a little human being that's sole purpose is to test our boundaries in order to learn about the world around them. You are doing a fabulous job momma!

GIN O'CLOCK

Is it almost time for gin I ask?
As I beg for the millionth time,
To get his school uniform on,
Surely 8 isn't too early for wine?

I often feel like I'm drowning,
After treading water for too long,
Everything always seems so hard,
I feel like I'm doing everything wrong!

If I were a knitted jumper,
I feel like I'm coming apart at the seams,
This isn't the idea of motherhood I had,
The idealistic bubble in my dreams,
Where are my picture-perfect moments?
Far and few in between,
Now I have a four-year-old,
Who is already acting like a teen.

Juggling work and being a mother,
The house is never clean,
I'm always so damn tired,
Cranky, bitchy and mean.

I know this time won't last forever,
I know it will get better,
Maybe I can really have it all
And be a #trendsetter.

But for now this is my reality,
Being covered in snot and I hope that's chocolate!
Doing the lively samba for now,
Until my time for the elegant foxtrot.

This poem is my truth,
It's how I often feel,
Like a fruit ready to be eaten,
Exposed, without its peel.

If you can relate to all that I've said,
Then I hope that you all know,
We've got this mommas,
And although we feel like amateurs,
To our children we are the pro!

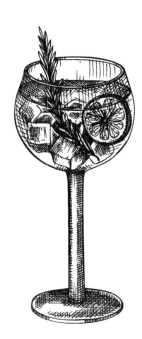

Who would like a position where you:

- May get pooed and/or urinated on
- Will get disturbed constantly through the night for reasons such as: Growing pains, vomit, fevers or just because sleeping is boring, to name a few.
- Will have to spend all your money on things that will get broken within about a minute of purchasing.
- Will become a chef for the most pickiest of eaters, who will literally throw their food at you for good measure.

anyone?
Did I mention the position is unpaid?

WHIRLWIND

That little chuckle,

That tiny curl

My clever boy,

My inquisitive girl.

They make me laugh,

They make me cry

They make me crash,

They make me fly,

They make me mad,

They make me proud,

They give me a headache,

When they are being too loud.

They make a mess,

They tidy up,

They make me feel

Like an overflowing cup.

My mixed emotions,

My roller coaster ride,

My wanting to run to the bathroom to hide.

Bathroom antics,

The flooded floor

Putting away those clothes,

That I've already put away before.

My greatest blessings,

They give such joy

My inquisitive girl

And my clever boy.

Nothing will ever prepare you for the changes your body goes through during and after pregnancy. I thought the hardest part would be child birth, how naïve I was...

POST PARTUM

Zumba Class,

Jump, one, two, three,

Shit, I just let out a little wee.

I did my Kegels,

But boy do I miss

Having a sneeze

Without a dribble of piss.

I never quite knew

What changes to expect,

But wearing Tena ladies daily,

Is quite hard to accept.

I do miss my old life,

Where I could choose to sleep in,

Before drinking a "hot" drink was considered a win.

Before date nights were properly scheduled months in advance,

And before the days where I didn't have to wear Bridget Jones' pants.

But despite all these things, the list I could write,

My children are my greatest and biggest delight.

I believe very strongly that Lockdown 2020 was a huge contributing factor to why my child is so feral at times. She was caged and yet longed for freedom that I couldn't give to her. Now I feel caged...but in the same cage as the lions.

THE CELL

These walls have become my prison,
My voice the warden's song,
For although I know inside
Is not where we all belong,
The outside world it terrifies
The outcomes out of my control,
For when I venture out with my babes
I feel they will swallow me whole.
With ignorance and indifference,
With wailing and flailing arms,
Even if I have my threats as defences
And my treats aimed to disarm.
The question remains is it today,
That I will drag myself to freedom?
No, we remain in our cell,
With the children in charge of the kingdom.

If you ever see a parent struggling with their child do's and don'ts:

Do ask if they need help (distraction for the child or hold parent's things if they are trying to hold child, even if its just to help them move somewhere more discreet).

Do say comments that make the parents know they are not alone in their battles. We have all been there...don't pretend it's never happened to you! Don't just stand and stare whilst passing your very obvious judgement.

TRENDS

If people were trends,
I'd be so last year,
Still hiding away from the world,
Lost in my fear.
If I go out with the kids,
Will they tantrum and shout?
Will they demand what they want?
With their stomping and pout?
Will I get all those looks?
You know the ones that I mean,
The ones intended to support,
But so often demean.
Do I ignore the behaviour,
Or do I call it out?
Do I just stay at home
And make do without?
Shut myself away,
From those disapproving glares,
When my children's wild behaviour
Catches me unawares.
I wish I knew the right thing to do,
To know the right thing to say,
Perhaps this mothering thing will get easier in time,
Perhaps...maybe...one day.

There is a lot of pressure to be the perfect social media mummy, who does everything right to get the gold stars for mummy school.
This is not the reality.

The reality is we lose ourselves; our identity is stripped and our body ravaged and we sometimes need a bit of time to grieve for that version of ourselves we will never be again. Take the time and do not feel guilty about it. No matter what anyone else says.

MOTHERHOOD

Motherhood,
Is to be understood
By so many women around us.
They feel our stresses,
They feel our strains,
But to persevere is a must.

For we have these little people,
Who rely on our every move,
And it's not to the whole world,
That we have anything to prove.

We just need to be there for them,
Whenever they need us most,
Even if that often means,
The pre-mother in us becomes a ghost.

I never quite realised what domesticated life would entail and the many tasks that it would come with...this is why women are amazing multi-taskers.

THE TO DO LIST

Tidy, fix, clean, cuddle,

Tell them not to jump in that muddy puddle.

Wipe, cook, feed, dress,

Tidy up yet another mess.

Console, reprimand, teach, love,

This list is not exhaustive from what's mentioned above.

What does it mean, these never ending tasks?

This is called being a mother; the wearer of many masks.

Not going to lie, sometimes my children's never ending questions really overwhelm my already pretty overwhelmed brain. Never feel guilty about finding escapes in those moments to regain your composure.

Some may proclaim that giving your child electronic devices is devil's work, but there is nothing devilish about giving them the means to answer their questions with CBeebies, to give yourself that 5 minutes that you need.

QUESTION TIME

What's this? What's that?
How come the earth's not flat?
How come? What for?
But I've never been there before!
I want that, no this,
Is this kid taking the piss?

I'm taking it in, I'm thinking it through,
I'm trying to find yet another activity to do,
Let's take a minute, some time to reflect,
I don't have to prove to my child that I'm perfect.

It's at times like this where I feel the need to apologise to my own mother...

A CAUTIONARY TALE

Now listen here and listen well,

For I have a story I wish to tell,

Of a time where I had the freedom to roam,

Without making sure there was an adult present at home.

The time before a cough or a sneeze,

Would let a dribble of wee out with such ease.

I love my children, love them to death,

But every once in a while, I need to catch my breath,

One of them is naked, screaming she wants to go in the pool,

The other one is taking 5 hours to get himself ready for school.

I don't regret having children, but life was simpler when,

I didn't need to leave my dinner to wipe someone's bum time and time again.

Now don't get me wrong they are magical and full of comedy gold,

But I swear since we became a family of 4, I'm feeling more grey and old.

So have kids of course, but please beware,

You'll never be as relaxed again unless they're asleep or in child care.

I never knew stubborn until I had my second born daughter Athena. With a will as strong as hers, there is nothing that girl will not achieve in her life. As for her poor mother...send gin!

STUBBORN CHILD OF MINE

It was a beautiful day,
No cause for alarm,
Unless you class the screaming child,
I'm currently trying to disarm.
I get it, the park is awesome,
with lots to do and see,
I thought it would be a nice adventure
Except its now ruled by tyranny.
My assertive voice isn't assertive,
My shout only leads her to giggle,
Picking her up to show it's time to go,
Causes her only to wriggle.
I offer her snacks,
I bribe her with juice,
I strap her into her pushchair
And within seconds she's loose.
I'm fighting a loosing battle,
Against this stubborn child of mine,
But if you were to ask me how I am,
You can bet me a fiver I'd say I was fine.

In the moment, it seems to last forever.
After it; time seems to fall away.

CHILD'S EYES

We've measured up the feet again,
I can't believe how much they've grown,
When I look into my child's eyes,
I feel like I am looking in my own.
The rate at which you're blooming,
From your hair down to your feet,
Has caught me by surprise, and
Almost knocked me off my feet.
I snap a million photos,
To hold you in this time,
To keep you as my baby,
The time when you were mine.
Because before I know it,
You'll be grown up and out the door,
Ready to take on the big wide world alone,
Eager to Explore.

Motherhood comes with a lot of external and internal pressures. When that pressure gets too much for you, take the weight off your feet, do something you enjoy and remember we are all just winging it.

MOTHER F***ING QUEEN

Legs flailing,
Feel like I'm failing,
Why is motherhood so hard?

Feel like I'm seething,
With every breath that I'm breathing,
Wish life came with an instruction card.

Routine daily,
Though never plain sailing,
Thank God for my online connections.

Motherhood is competition,
The Insta grid mummy's mission,
To always appear without imperfections.

I keep it real,
To show how I feel,
So that you know you are never alone.

So even on dark days,
You can see the light in other ways,
As I remind you, you're the queen on the throne.

I was not prepared for how much camomile lotion I would have to use on such a small person.

CONSTELLATION

If I could create a constellation
And what it really meant,
It be would be the figure of someone strong
Not a god, but of a parent.
The dreaded pox has invaded,
And with it, it has brought,
Itchy and irritable children,
From this dreaded illness caught.
One just wanted cuddles,
The other please don't touch,
Covering them with camomile,
Even though it looks too much.

Calpol is our saviour,
Shower times are the best,
I look forward to those bed times,
To finally get some rest.
And then it's morning once again,
The day will start anew,
I'm praying for a better day,
With strength to see it through.
So if you see a parent,
Frazzled and unkempt,
Just think of how their day has gone,
And please hold any judgment.

Since having children I definitely do not feel in charge anymore!

IGOR

Master, master please let me rest,

I'm trying to do my very best.

Master, master I will make you some lunch,

Even though I've literally just given you something to munch.

Master, master, I'm sorry, I'm trying,

Please oh please, will you just stop crying.

Master, Master, I'm trying to help you,

I would rather not be covered in your wee or poo.

Master, master please let me sleep,

It's the only part of my sanity, I really need to keep.

My master, my baby, sleeping soundly at last,

Better drink my cuppa, do the ironing and eat something fast!

The 5pm lull of waiting for the hubby to get home because I've had enough of adulting for one day!

HONEY, I'M HOME

Long day at work;
Blood sweat and tears,
The baby is screaming again,
Igniting all my mummy fears.

The 4 year old won't eat his tea,
He's causing quite a scene,
I'm trying to use my mummy shout,
Without coming across too mean.

There's washing and ironing mounting up,
I feel like I'm coming undone,
Have kids, they say, it's amazing, they say,
This isn't my idea of fun!

It's nearly bed time, oh thank the lord,
All I seem to do is moan,
Until the moment the husband arrives,
Shouting to me "honey, I'm home!"

If a parent is offloading how difficult it has been for them, please think twice before replying with how bad you had it. Let them get it off their chest without having to compete for who had it worst. Our battles are each our own and we all handle them in different ways. Give them that time to understand that you know it's hard and that they are doing a great job, despite how they feel.

VALIDATION

I'm at the end of my tether,
I'm pulling out my hair
I'm sick of shouting at them to stop
And they don't even seem to care.

Some days I feel like screaming,
Screaming for it all to stop,
When I talk to people about how I feel,
They say I'm being over the top.

They say "It's like you're the only one who's got children,
Some have it harder than you",
And of course I do appreciate that,
But I need validating too.

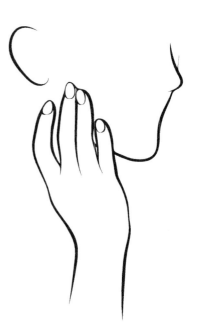

Lockdown 2020 really did a number on us as a family. Isolating from freedom and our usual familial support. We got through it though, not unscathed, but definitely having learnt more patience and how to juggle what seemed impossible.

LOCKED UP

The days have moulded in one long nightmare,
Of phonics, Numberblocks and tantrums,
How much longer will I have to endure,
These annoying Jack Hartmann anthems?
Mom guilt persisting,
Wine drinking resisting,
At least before 7pm.
And then wake up in the morning,
New day is dawning,
And I get to do it all over again.
My waist line expands,
As every Thursday we clap our hands,
And essentials have become chocolate and booze.
But at least on the Bright side,
without the darn school run,
Can set that old alarm back to snooze…

Oh wait we have young children,
And rest is a rare commodity,
Trying to convince the 4 year old
To follow the social distancing policy.
I suppose it's not all doom and gloom,
Families are spending more time together,
Feeling like the cast of big brother or love island,
Out in the garden soaking up any of the good weather.
We miss our families, more and more everyday,
We facetime and drop shopping at their front door
Just showing them our love in whatever way,
Too scared to risk them going in a store.
All these moments in isolation,
Hoping to receive quotes or cards with inspiration,
Positive thoughts, funny memes, TikToks coming from everywhere
Rainbow spotting, bear hunting, chalking the pavements without a care,
In this rare occasion we are all equal in our fear,
United by a common threat,
Even when all this nightmare has come to an end,
Our generation will never forget.

Lockdown 2020,
Keyworkers risking endlessly,
Themselves and their families,
Of this deadly viral calamity,
I wish you safe and I wish you well,
And Covid-19,
you can go to hell!

Our children are the gifts that keeps on giving; and we should never look a gift horse in the mouth.

THE GIFT

I see the sparkle in your eyes,
When I tell you the surprise,
Your fists clench in pure excitement,
You're an angel in disguise.

Disguised as my daughter,
I could drink you up like water,
I trace your face with my finger,
You the story, me the author.

I see the wonder of all of you,
I know my love for you is true,
My heart fell in love before our eyes did meet,
You are the gift that I grew,
And could not wait to greet.

The phrase "Don't cry over spilt/spilled milk" is the contemporary variation of the idiom "No weeping for shed milk", originally published in 1659 by James Howell. A man clearly unfamiliar with the concept of the pump and dump.

PUMP AND DUMP

To many this concept is foreign,
But any breastfeeding mother will know,
That their precious liquid gold is too valuable,
To ever want to let it go.

But if ever you wanted a tipple,
Or you're away from your baby too long,
You know pumping your milk is the only way,
To negate the pain you don't wish to prolong.

The pain that says they are fit for bursting,
That it's got to be drunk or pumped away,
And if you don't have the capabilities of storage,
Then unfortunately that milk cannot stay.

The pump and dump can be the only solution,
And there's many a tear I have cried,
After pumping what my body amazingly creates,
and throwing down the sink, dying inside.

For some, milk supply is in abundance,
For others they've worked hard for that ounce,
And it doesn't matter how much we must dump,
It would hurt in any amount.

They say don't cry over spilt milk
And no shock that's a man's invention,
But say it to a mother whose pumped and dumped
And you may need to seek medical attention.

It's really hard to stop yourself from becoming a helicopter parent, especially if you had one yourself. You need to let your kids know that it's safe to explore without you, but that you will always be their anchor and they can draw you in when they need you.

HELICOPTER PARENT

She hovers over you,
Protecting by any means,
Making sure you're having fun,
But not in front of screens,
Which means as it turns out,
Exploring the great outdoors,
With her getting anxious,
In case of sudden downpours.

She makes sure she has provisions,
But what if there's something she's missed?
She keeps stocking up the nappy bag,
And ticking off the to-do list.

She watches over as you play,
Never straying too far,
The time before when you hurt yourself,
Had left an emotional scar.

So now she is a helicopter parent,
She feels so uncertain and unsure,
Knowing she is possibly limiting your flight,
When she should be letting you soar.

Think back to a time when you were younger...do you remember your own comfort toy?

THE COMFORT TOY

We all want our child to find comfort,
We buy them comforters, blankets and toys,
We give in to dummies, CBeebies and Alexa,
Anything to help bring them joy.

We want them to have that one thing,
That they want and need just as much as us,
Something snuggly that we have lovingly bought for them,
Something small and easily carried is a plus.

But what happens when they cling to it,
Despite it needing a wash,
When it's now covered in snot and Nutella,
And you've accidently used it to wipe up your squash.

You now won't accept a replacement,
Your comforter you cry for at night,
And when you are presented with it all clean again,
I witness your absolute delight.

You kiss and cuddle it when going to nursery,
You treat it like it's a real thing,
And no matter where we are going,
It's an item you always need to bring.

Of all the things we've ever bought you,
This simple pleasure has taken your heart,
So we always try and make sure that,
You and hungry caterpillar are rarely apart.

I have two fussy eaters, but I'll be honest, this is very much karma for me.

THE FUSSY EATER

I have a fussy eater,
And although I've tried and tried,
To get you to munch,
Something green for your lunch,
You prefer something greasy and fried.

I have a fussy eater,
I beg you to take a bite,
Just give it a try,
There's no need to cry,
But every mealtime is just one big fight.

I have a fussy eater,
My freezer full of food,
But it's only nuggets,
You want in your guts,
And if I refuse, you'll be in a bad mood.

I have a fussy eater,
And because you don't have 5 a day,
Your guts in a twist,
And needs medical assist,
But kids always have to learn the hard way.

There are so many firsts we get to be a part of. I'm so lucky I got to be the first woman to love you

THE FIRST

The first time you opened your eyes,
I saw into your soul,
The first time I held you close,
I felt I was made whole.
The first time you made a noise,
Was to mine and your delight,
The first time you rolled over,
You gave yourself a nasty fright.

The first time you were able to crawl,
I knew this would mean trouble,
The first time you tried to stand,
I wanted to wrap you in a protective bubble.
The first time you took a step,
I didn't know my heart could be prouder,
The first time you said my name,
Then continued to keep saying it louder.

The first time I left you at nursery,
Was difficult, but you started to thrive,
The first time you lived through a pandemic,
Was scary, but we all survived.
The first time you welcomed your sister,
You held her tightly in your arms,
The first time she started to cry,
You found her dummy, knowing it calms.

The first time you told a lie,
And we talked about the importance of truth,
The first time you blamed your sister,
And we talked about the boy that cried wolf.

There have been so many firsts,
With you my first born,
And although that time has passed,
There's no need for me to mourn.
Every first is captured in my memory,
It makes me smile just to recall,
My now grown up first born boy,
Who started off life being oh so small.

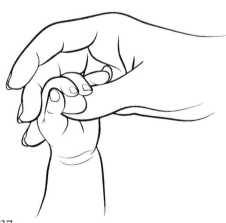

To Deb, Maddie, Karen, Sian and all the amazing women from Home-start NE Worcestershire. You helped me through a dark period in my life and continue to support me with your kindness and understanding. I hate to think what would have happened if you hadn't been there to reach out to. For anyone who is feeling lost there are so many places you can reach out to. Charities who will talk to you, support you and signpost you to the specific help you need. Never feel ashamed to ask for help.

MORE THAN JUST BABY BLUES

I had this idea,

This feeling of what motherhood should be,

Filled with lots of baby cuddles and a warm feeling of ecstasy.

But my journey into motherhood,

Did not feel like this,

Instead of pure elation, I felt myself floating in the abyss.

I felt overwhelmed by the weight of it all,

The responsibility I now had,

I felt like I was coming undone and slowly going mad.

I felt hopeless and lost,

Holding a baby as if a weight,

Whilst I'm swimming against the currents, waiting for the life vest to inflate.

But it doesn't inflate,

It's faulty, and instead I'm drowning in your cries,

And each day that passes, another part of myself slowly dies.

These feelings were not fleeting,

They grew as time moved on,

And when I was at my lowest ebb, I thought the old me had completely gone.

This was more than just baby blues,

This was something I could not dismiss,

My face aflame with shame, my heart locked within a furnace.

I reached out and received,

The help I needed in order to cope,

My local Home-Start; the charity, that began to bring back my hope.

They showed me there was a light,

At the end of this dark tunnel I was lost in,

And the first step was acknowledging, I needed my healing to begin.

To find the root of the problem,

To validate the pain that I felt,

To soothe my inner child, whom in the darkness dwelt.

The countdown clock to the summer holidays or any school holiday in fact chimes very loud in my head. A time of still trying to work from home, take care of the house whilst it is continually being destroyed and stop two siblings from beating each other up.

THE SUMMER BREAK...DOWN

I feel it coming,
My breath catches in my throat,
Summer is here,
Every parent in the same boat.
Trying to entertain my children,
Whilst still trying to work,
Finding limitless activities,
Whilst the housework, I must shirk.
For it's now near enough impossible,
To keep the house in a respectable state,
Whilst I keep staring ahead,
At the September school start date.

I can do this, I tell myself,
As I scour the Facebook pages,
For fun activities I can do on the cheap,
Suitable for multiple ages.
I draw a blank, the park it is,
Everyone else had the same idea,
Maybe we can go and play house,
Kill a couple of hours in IKEA,
Go for meatballs, what time is it now?
Are you *joking* its only gone ten?
And now we're back home and staring
At the television screen once again.

I hear an argument begin to erupt,
Between my son and daughter,
I decide let's get the pool out,
That takes two hours to fill up with water.
Two hours then pass,
And it's time to play,
They are loving it,
I am never putting this thing away.
They are engaged and having fun,
I stop to make a gin,
Thinking this is finally when
Our summer holidays begin.
Of course they find a sharp branch,
And within seconds the pool has collapsed
Me trying to figure out,
How much time their fun elapsed.

Its twelve O'clock, so time for lunch,
As my picky eaters choose,
I make them what they ask for of course,
But of course my daughter will refuse.
We do colouring, play board games,
Kick a ball around to each other,
We have a tantrum about sharing again,
As little miss no longer wants a brother,
This groundhog day, that seems never-ending,
Is nearly done with, I think,
When I hear the front door open for Daddy,
Only another 41 days in the clink.

For Theo and Athena,

No matter how hard it gets,
No matter the pain we go through,
Nothing beats being a mother,
To two children like you.

Love mommy xxx

LIFE'S LITTLE MIRACLE

There have been so many times I've felt lost,
That waves of overwhelm have engulfed me,
With you and your brother always arguing,
And me having to act as referee.

But then there are moments of pure joy,
I look at you and you look at me,
And a pang of love fills my heart,
In a way I could never foresee.

For nothing prepares you for having children,
Not even a childcare diploma did that job,
That although I knew all the basics,
I didn't know you could make my heart throb.

It hits me so unexpected,
That pride and love combined,
When I watch you playing with your friends,
Or when you do or say something kind.

When you are fast asleep in your bed,
And I'm watching your chest rise and fall,
It takes me back to the time before,
When you were a baby so helpless and small.

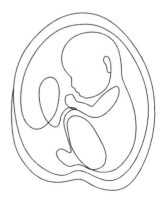

It's these moments I need to draw back onto,
When the hard times are taking its toll,
You are one of life's little miracles,
And your happiness is my only goal.

Life gives us many lessons and it will often keep giving us the same one until we learn from it.

SOCIAL LESSONS

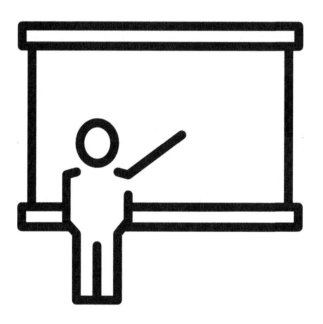

SOCIAL LESSONS

Throughout our lives we are continually learning lessons. How we behave in an ever changing world. A world where we spend more and more time on electronic devices than ever before. A world where bullying and trolling can follow us wherever we go and a world where we have grown less and less tolerant of others and their differences. Maybe its the global pandemic, the stress of economy crashes and even war that drives us humans at times to behave in ways and say things that are just not nice. A behaviour we have now named 'Karen' (sorry to all the lovely Karen's out there). This chapter focuses on the lessons I have witnessed in the past few years. From the #bekind movement that so often gets forgotten when it really counts, post Covid living, stories that I've encountered in the press and those with social media dependency, (myself included).

In my own head, I live in a world that is sunshine and rainbows, full of unicorns and mermaids and sparkles and the darkness that has spread to so many makes me so genuinely scared for my own children. What sort of life will they have if they are continually being subjected to create labels that define the very being they are? These poems are my dream of a mass wake up call to the negatively impacting messages we are seeing portrayed in the media all the time. This is my war cry for kindness and compassion and fairness.

I hope these poems open your eyes and inspire you to be the very best version of yourself!

LIKE, FOLLOW, SHARE

This life is all we get,
We have to make it count,
And it's really not defined
By your follower amount.
No one cares if you went viral,
No one really knows the truth,
Of who you really are in life,
Social Media is not your proof.
So stand up and make a difference,
Engage in real life affairs,
Do random acts of kindness,
But not for likes and shares.
Be present in the moment,
Remove the past and future
Use your voice to stand for good,
Away from the computer.
Because this life is all we get,
And we have to make it count,
And the flesh and bone version of you,
Is so much better than your online account.

Many a time I have found myself in a
comment battle on Facebook.
Trying to defend someone who is being
ripped to shreds,
Just to put myself in the firing line
instead.

HOW DARE YOU

I try not to offend,
But nowadays it's a minefield,
For every word I may say,
Could be a sword I wield.
Against an online troll,
Who is allowed their own opinion,
But if I have one of my own,
I'm reminded I'm in their dominion.
So although I state my differing point,
With mindful thought and tact,
An opinion is neither right nor wrong,
As it's not based on actual fact.
So just because you don't agree,
With what someone has to say,
We don't have to spout out hate,
There is always a better way.

Loosely inspired by the events at the end of the 2000 film 'Pay it forward', where fighting bullies, the main protagonist is left mortally wounded by a switchblade.

There are always so many things that lead to moments like this, both within fiction and in the real world. We need to make sure we have both of our eyes and our hearts open to see it and stop it, before it's too late.

PAY CLOSE ATTENTION

If you pay close attention,
To how a magician does a trick,
You can see how they may do it,
Although it may be quick.

If you pay close attention
You will notice the cloud shapes in the sky,
Transforming with every gust of wind,
As you gently walk on by.

If you pay close attention
You will spot a group of ants,
Walking from the picnic table,
And back towards the plants.

If you pay close attention,
You will notice the birds are singing,
The baby bird yearns greedily,
For more worms their parent is bringing.

If you pay close attention,
You may just see a tear,
Fall from a youth's eye,
As they hide away in fear.
You may notice that a bruise
Is growing on their arm,
And you may even start to wonder,
Who would want to do them harm?

But you didn't pay close attention,
And the punch became a knife,
And the bruises turned to gushing blood
As another teen lost their life.
All the signs had been there,
And a bully will never stop,
Till everyone is beneath them
So they are the only one left on top.

Pipe down Karen!

OPINIONS

Opinions are like assholes,
We've all got one of our own,
Don't be afraid to voice them,
But maybe not just from your mobile phone.
Embark in political debate
Hash out the pros and cons
But learn when to stop and listen,
Rather than dropping hateful words like bombs.
They feel safe behind their screens,
Without accountability for their typing,
Disagreeing with what everyone says
If it's not to their personal liking.
We need to put more kindness out,
Into this world that we all share,
So please do have your opinions,
But express them with some thought and care.

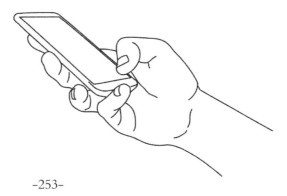

The more I scroll through social media, the more I realise I may not be seeing a person's genuine face. Authenticity is beautiful, it's real. Although there is a time and a place for a filter, we should never be using one to replace our own reflection because we don't feel that our reflection is good enough. It is more than enough!

FILTER

Can we smooth out all the lines
Add a filter to contour and shape?
Add makeup we couldn't bother to apply,
And plaster on a smile that's fake.
Let's change up the hair colour,
And why not the eye colour too,
Don't you look so much better
With eyes that are baby blue?
Everything just looks better
Because nothing resembles you.
And people will think that's how you look,
Save a select close few
You can hide behind the filter,
That makes you feel perfect,
But all you're doing is hurting,
From yourself you disconnect.
So no matter hard it may be,
Remove the filter from your face,
And surround yourself with authenticity,
To create a non-toxic space.

Being bullied is a lonely path to walk down, but not a path we walk down alone.

THOUGHTS OF YOU

When I was but a girl, naïve and quite shy,
Another took pleasure in making me cry,
She pushed and she taunted, she ganged up on me and
She told others to exclude me when I held out my hand.
She ruled the school as queen, and I as the joker,
Firing insults that penetrated my skin like a poker.
The animal in me just wanted to choke her,
For the pain she inflicted filled my lungs like a smoker.
I didn't fight for myself, I was not that way inclined,
And my confidence and happiness each day at school declined.

She manipulated and lied and made me feel so alone,
She was the enemy who charged forward, making her presence known
I spent years feeling hate, when now I understand,
It wasn't me that she hated, it was herself she couldn't stand.
Dealing with identity issues and sexuality too,
Her frustrations reverberated to anyone who,
Made her feel insecure, who made her question herself,
The hate that she spawned, was her own cry for help.

But at the age of 7, how was I to see,
That this girl who was so cruel actually needed me.
She ruined my childhood and gave me so many issues,
But we don't know how it feels to walk in someone else's shoes.
Now as an adult I can revisit and heal,
Imagine how that 7 year old girl used to feel.
It's not anger I feel now, but pity instead,
For a girl so angry at life she only saw red.
But my bully became my own inner voice, one that I wish to silence,
And I have to push past the feelings of self hate as my own final act of defiance.
Because I was never the problem, the things I told myself were not true,
And these are the lessons that come to my mind, when I'm having my thoughts of you.

It's all too easy to lose sight of the right path when we get overwhelmed by the many paths presented to us. Just listen to your heart and know it will guide you

TRUST IS EARNT

Trust in actions, not in words,

Actions can not be misheard,

Words can be twisted, misconstrued, manipulated,

Meanings often anticipated,

So we jump to our own conclusions,

Make up scenarios that can be delusions.

Life isn't black and white,

We won't always get it right

There's never the need to fight,

If we view things with love in our sight.

Do you remember all those horror
films about robots
taking over the world?
What is more scary is that it would have
all started with a computer.

HELLO PAST SELF

Hello past self, it's me from the future,
Telling you about life after the computer.
We live our lives behind a screen or within an app,
From nature and true connection, we've taken a nap.
We define ourselves from the photos on our feed or grid,
We'd sell our soul on the marketplace for a couple of quid.
We live in a constant battle between acceptance and denial,
All the while trying to plaster on our best smile,
To show the outside world that inside we're not broken,
A like or thumbs up our most treasured token.
We put out only what we want others to know,
So they can sit back and relax and enjoy the show.
But none of it's real, it's all smokes and mirrors,
Thinking how life is turning out, gives me the shivers.
So wake up now before it's too late,
Life behind a screen doesn't need to be your fate.

This goes out to my good friends at middle school Zakk Chambers, Niall Kerrins and Peter Dunton who took me under their wings in year 7 when on the playground. We enacted scenes from Star wars: Attack of the Clones, in which I played Padmé Amidala. And not forgetting the great Harry Potter... We had such a blast!

STUCK IN THE MIDDLE

When I was at school they called me gay,
For wanting to show affection in my own way
I was a hugger, what can I say?
But teasing me about it, was not okay.
I remember the days I stayed in to read,
With my teachers and prefects I often would plead,
For the playground is where hate can often breed,
But within my fiction I felt happy and freed.
I was always trying hard to find my place,
Not always content with having my space,
Then there was the moment I saw your face,
And loneliness was now never the case.
You let me join in with your fun and games,
Pretending and make believe were our playground aims,
We would recreate our favourite films frame by frame,
Now it's just my memories of these moments that remain.
Middle school antics,
Hopeless romantics,
Spin the bottle
Truth and dare
Adding to the dramatics.
These were the days,
The days of our youth,
Where we hadn't been broken down
By the weight of the truth.
That although we resisted,
Our pre-teen days consisted
Of fun that has now twisted
Into adulthood.

I have gotten so cross when someone has said to me that it's good that my husband is babysitting the kids, when I've been out. No, he isn't babysitting, he is parenting. It is a joint role that we share because we BOTH made the decision to have children. I am so sick to death of the expectations that women need to be everything to everyone all of the time without breaking a sweat. We need to keep speaking up about this bullshit until enough people are listening!

MOTHER SHOULD

Motherhood, all mothers would,
Take care of her children and work as she should,
Taking care of her home and her partner too,
Whilst spending time needing to cry on the loo.

Work like you don't have kids,
Have kids like you don't work,
Is the expectation many have,
Which I think is berserk.

Bring in a good wage,
Raise productive offspring,
Be pillars of the community,
Be good at everything.

The expectation of women,
Is to never bend or break,
But how can we carry on like this?
We can't for god's sake!

Women aren't only caregivers,
We aren't the only ones to clean,
And just because we are being assertive,
Doesn't make us bitchy or mean.

We don't have to do the cooking
And we can certainly produce our own pleasure,
And unlike our male counterparts,
It's not our dicks we measure.

Yet our role in society is dictated,
By the patriarchy who don't respect,
How a mother's love and fierceness,
Is more powerful than you can expect.

Being a mother is a job on its own,
We shouldn't feel the guilt to be,
Every other role there is to be had,
One day the men will see.

I really struggle with time management and find myself stuck in the death scroll on social media that wipes out hours of my life, without having achieved anything remotely substantial.

TICK TOCK

Time is an illusion,
We think we have it to spare,
But our time is only important,
If we spend it with those we care.
In a world where we can be anything,
We are told we should always be kind,
But trolls linger in their online caves,
With words that try to bind
Us to their negative viewpoint,
Of a world where they see no hope,
Picking everything we say and do apart,
Putting us under a microscope.
Dissecting every decision,
Judge jury and and the cancel culture
They prey on every failure we make,
Waiting for death like a hungry vulture.
These harbingers of death and grief,
These hateful fundamentalists,
Make us waste our precious time scrolling,
This is time's ultimate nemesis.
So if you want to win the battle,
Do yourself a favour,
Delete, block and move on
That's how to be time's saviour.

This poem is written post Covid. My doctor's surgery have a first stage doctor appointment via the phone, no matter what the ailment is. This has often led to delays in getting the care we need. Most of the time prescription medication has been thrown at us that has not helped the problem, because we needed to be seen, to be properly diagnosed. After my husband's third set of antibiotics for an ear infection, he went to the out of hours, who said the medication he was on was for an inner ear infection, whereas he had an outer ear infection. The doctor at the clinic could not fathom why our surgery refused to make a face to face appointment, despite my husband asking for one.

PRESS 2 FOR APPOINTMENTS

I need to see my doctor,
I need an appointment because,
My back's in tatters, I can barely walk,
And my head's feeling all a fuzz.

I need to see my doctor,
Because my mental health is a mess,
I'm feeling unstable,
And not mentally able,
To even sometimes get myself dressed.

I need to see my doctor,
I can't quite shake this feeling,
That something's not right,
But I don't have the fight,
To chat on the phone is just not appealing.

I need to see my doctor,
But they don't want to see me,
For every time I ring up,
It's my own reflection that I see,
As I stare at the living corpse in the mirror,
As once again I pace on the phone,
My doctor not wanting to see me,
As it's easier for them when I'm home.

I want to see my doctor,
Because a doctor cannot diagnose,
When on the other end of the line,
They do try though I suppose.

Give them this, and maybe try that,
As my prescription bill gets ever higher,
To afford the amount of pills I'm on,
I need to be an economic highflyer.

Pills are sometimes the answer,
But sometimes maybe they're not,
But because you refuse to see your patients,
We just feel like we are being left to rot.

And I know being a doctor is no picnic,
There's pressures that I'll never know,
But it's your job to take care of us,
And we feel like we've all been let go.

So bring back your face to face appointments,
Don't make us beg to be seen,
Because being able to see your doctor,
Should be a normal day to day routine.

This poem was written in the wake of the suicide of Caroline Flack in 2020, when #bekind was at its peak. I wanted to bring to light how detrimental online bullying can be.

EMPTY CHAIR AT THE TABLE

"Oh my gosh have you seen this?
This video is so funny,
Look at the clothes this kid is wearing,
They must not have any money.
I'm going to comment, everyone else has,
And say something really witty,
Were you blind when you got dressed this morning? Your fashion sense is shitty!
In fact being blind for you would be a blessing,
Then at least you would have an excuse for your crappy dressing
And while you're at it, a bag for your head…"
The kid read the comments and wished he was dead.
He scrolled through the hate, his innocent post had procured,
His face behind the screen, from his parents was obscured.

He didn't want them to see him as a tear rolled down his cheek,
If his dad saw him crying he would only call him weak.
He just wanted to show the world, what he was all about,
That just like all the girls out there, he too could do a good pout.
He wanted to create something funny, just like his mates at school,
And then the world of social media would stop and think he was cool,
But now he sees the backlash and he just feels like a fool,
He never realised that the world, could be so very cruel.
Sitting behind their phone screens, knowing there are no defences,
They troll and comment hatefully without knowing the consequences.
The kid goes up to his room, to do his homework he says,
And after taking all the pills he could find, on his bed he lays.

Sometimes we just need to get it all off
our chest in a good old rant!

BARK

I don't recognise the bark of my voice
The sound so shrill it pierces ears,
It tries to make commands with it,
And demands respect and fear.

It's a voice that seems so foreign,
So far removed from the one I've known,
Is this what happens to us,
When our voice is fully grown?

I miss singing sweet melodies,
Without a care of the pitch or tone,
Before the days where your judgement,
Came from a Karen sitting at home on her phone.

The bark of my voice is angry,
It wishes so much to be heard,
Shouting how the state of the world is a shambles,
How our governments decisions are absurd.

How we can't #bekind to each other,
Unless someone loses their life,
And the era of political correctness gone awry,
Means more online rants and ravings are rife.

I'm sorry if this poem offends you,
But I too deserve to be heard,
But I won't add to the barking rhetoric
I will sing with my written word.

This poem was written after not one but two Instagram accounts within a week of each other tried to scam me using the sugar daddy scam. I decided to try and catch one out and lo and behold money was "sent" to my PayPal email but needed a bitcoin payment to release. The email I was sent to many would have looked totally legitimate, luckily I don't trust anyone on the internet.

IF SOMETHING SOUNDS TOO GOOD TO BE TRUE...

You get into my DMs,
Trying to sell me this amazing dream,
Of riches that you'll send to me,
But this is not what it would seem.
You promise me a fortune,
In exchange for something small,
But you don't want to give anything away,
Your mission is to take it all.
You pray on the vulnerable,
Those who need your assistance,
Those who won't ask too many questions,
Or meet you with resistance.

You sell them a solution
To all the problems they confess,
And then leave them all miserable
And in an even bigger mess.
You've left families in ruin,
And children without a home,
All because you know how
To be savvy on the end of a mobile phone.
You are absolute pieces of shit,
Tracking down desperate people is a must,
So you can take all that they have, or don't,
By gaining all of their trust.

You use names they would recognise,
In emails that look legit,
Then use all their information,
And with their money, you do a flit.
There are many words to call you,
You vile corrupters and life destroyers,
You are a scammer,
The very worse of humanity's exploiters.
But there is one solution
To stop these villains on their path,
If something seems too good to be true,
Come on, you can do the math.

As a small business owner of a handmade business I have often been subjected to people questioning my pricing and feel that you need to work for free to make any sales.

This is a poem that acts as a gentle reminder of what us small business owners have to go through on a day to day basis and how people can support us.

PRICELESS

Wrapped up in words,

Entangled with rhyme,

Making money from art,

Has become such a crime.

You charge what it's worth,

You charge for your time,

Trying to make something of your talent,

Though the path is a climb.

Some say you're too cheap,

Others not cheap enough,

Who knew running a creative business,

Would be this tough?

You put yourself out there,

For the whole world to see,

And hope beyond hope,

Your art fills them with glee.

For every wax melt,

Candle and jewellery maker,

Decoupage, artist and painter,

You see the world with a different sight,

Breathing life into nothing

And giving it light.

What is that worth to capture that treasure?

It's priceless I say, something you cannot measure.

So don't haggle or scoff when they mention a price,

Admire their hard work is my only advice.

The more I scrolled through social media, the more I watched the news, the more I become outraged with how women are treated as pieces of meat. Where getting dressed up for a night out means a woman is inadvertently advertising that she is up for it? I think not!

ONE LUCKY GIRL

Is my short skirt an invitation,
Begging you to come inside?
Is my cleavage out on show,
Something I must hide?
If I want to avoid your wandering eyes,
And even your wandering hands,
Which sees me as an all you can eat buffet,
Your very own supply and demand.
We get labelled as tarts and sluts,
Even when we are saying 'No',
We try and have a good time with our friends,
And wish you would fuck off and go.
Stop grinding on my ass,
And thinking you've got a shot,
Do I have a sign that says please touch on my back,
That I somehow simply forgot?
And yeah, maybe I enjoy sexy dancing,
So you think of me as a tease,
But my body is mine alone to enjoy,
And the one I consent with to please.
So don't take what is not yours and retort,
That I was asking for it with what I was wearing,
Because all young boys should be taught,
How to not be sexually violent and overbearing.
To stop women despairing and continually repairing,
The damage one man can inflict,
Just because you thought I was one lucky girl,
That your sex depraved eyes had picked.

This poem is based on the Daily Mail article about the murder of Emma Pattison and her 7-year-old daughter by the hands of her husband George Pattison at Epsom College. The article chose to go down the line of trying to give the man a reason for doing what he did and of course, the speculations are that because his wife was a successful headteacher and family breadwinner, it was that, that drove him to murder.

SEXIST PROPAGANDA

I read in the paper a woman's been murdered,
Her husband shot her and her daughter dead,
But the headline reads "Did living in the shadows of his high achieving wife
Lead to unthinking tragedy" instead.

Is this what it's come to, where news blurs the lines,
Between what's an acceptable reason to murder?
That because a woman emasculates or wounds the male ego,
That gives him the right to hurt her?

Be careful women, you must stay in your place,
In case the big bad wolf comes a blowin',
But if your man can't accept a woman's power in this world,
Then girl you had better get going.

Do not play the part of cannon fodder,
Or a punchbag for a man's insecurity,
Find a man who respects your strength,
And shows a level of maturity.

Shame on those who choose to highlight,
A woman's success as her own downfall,
We need to change the stance on violence against women,
Instead of banging our head against a brick wall.

So change the fricking headline,
A murdering scumbag is all he is,
And women who work hard for success,
Are in danger whilst this propaganda lives.

Society has so many labels now that defines us. I don't judge anyone by their pre-picked labels, I judge based on what kind of person you are and how kind your heart is.

WHEN YOU ASSUME...

Does the colour of your skin really matter,

When all is said and done?

Does the fact that you are in a wheelchair,

Stop you from having fun?

Does who you love cause an issue,

To anyone but yourself?

Does having a modest budget,

Mean you aren't a family of wealth?

If your brain works a little differently,

Does it mean you must be excluded?

Or does it offer us another insight,

To roles that you would be better suited?

Our differences make us beautiful,

It's what sets us apart,

Whether its colour, sex or disability,

We need to make a start,

Of blocking out the bullshit

Passed down from generations of bigotry,

What we've been told by so many before,

Is nothing more than trickery.

So before you make assumptions,

On someone who is different to you,

Stop before you open your mouth,

And question, but is that thought actually true?

I don't watch the news anymore,
It's stories do nothing but depress.
Someone else murdered, a disaster
unleashed,
watching just makes me stressed!

THE WORLD AS WE KNOW IT

The world as we know it will cease to exist,

For in our ways of living we are firmly fixed.

We take more than we need,

And we don't share the wealth,

We bang on about #bekind,

Whilst destroying our own mental health,

By scrolling and fixating that our lives are a mess,

Compared to everyone else's Insta stories success.

I cannot express enough how much this distress

Lies squarely on the shoulders of those who wish to possess,

More, always wanting more,

And not love and understanding,

But things bought from a store.

I can't ignore, that where once there was a person, there isn't anymore,

Instead a self checkout kiosk is now fixed to the floor.

What the hell is going on, when the state of the world,

Is another sex exploitation conspiracy unfurled?

That we continue to find labels for every difference we own,

Thinking somehow this label will make us feel less alone.

But we treat ourselves like baggage,

Waiting to be reclaimed,

We wear our labels like a badge of honour,

To show we aren't ashamed,

But we don't need them,

Not really,

This label won't make others see us more clearly.

It's self acceptance, that's all that matters,

And showing our appreciation in more than being hand clappers,

Supporting our workers to fight for their rights,

Choosing to ignore hateful rhetoric which only ignites,

More hate and segregation,

In this already divided nation.

As we begin another year at the very brink of inflation,

Leaving the 'great' in Great Britain a rather boastful classification,

But this situation of taking more than we give,

Is something our future generations will not tolerate to forgive.

Sometimes we need to click reset and re-evaluate what is important in our lives.

RESET OF REALITY

With everything the way it is,
I stop and click reset,
I think it's really important
To have a reality check.
It's the norm to do your talking
On phones and over zooms,
To text your partner or children,
In the same house, but a different room.
It's the norm to spend more time,
In front of a screen and not a face,
As we make our big world smaller,
With online interactions tracked and traced.
We can value each other's comments
With a thumbs up or smiley emoji,
And if we don't get the engagement we seek,
We can start to deem ourselves unworthy.
We seek so much outside validation,
But I think it's important we see,
That we don't need other's approval,
To live a life that is happy and free.

thank ♥ you

FOR READING

If you love what you have read, leave a review for me on Amazon by searching Life and Rhymes and if you want to spread some extra love then come and leave a review on my Facebook page **@AthenasBountyuk** or follow me on Instagram **@athenas.bounty**. I also have a page dedicated to all things poetry **@nataliecarrpoetry** on both Facebook and Instagram.

If you love the idea of using poetry to help aid your own mental health recovery then come along and join my group **@TheBountyBunch** on Facebook. Within this group I will be hosting poetry events and workshops both online and in person as well as being able to keep up to date with what is happening within my wider business.

Check out the website **www.athenasbounty.co.uk**
YouTube: **@nataliesbountybunch**
Tik Tok: **@athenasountyuk**
I also have a podcast, new episodes coming soon! Check out **The Bounty Bunch Podcast** available on Amazon Music, Spotify and other music streaming platforms.

For any enquiries or to ask about commissioning a poem please email:
natalie@athenasbounty.co.uk

ACKNOWLEDGMENTS

There are a lot of people that I would like to thank for making this book happen. It's been a long time coming and an emotional rollercoaster to get to this point. I spent years worrying about what people would think if they were to read some of my darker material. So firstly, I would like to thank the woman whom I met at one of my markets. She told me her daughter felt broken which is why she was purchasing one of my magnetic mantra packs, and something told me to share the poem I had written only a few days before; 'Broken'. She asked me to send it to her because she felt her daughter needed to hear my words. My words were how she had been feeling and it was in that moment I knew I had to write this book, because although a dark poem, it made one person feel less alone in their battle, and that is my only goal with these poems.

I would like to thank my mother Susanne, who has always believed in me and my poetry and encouraged it since I began my journey with words. She herself has a knack for poetry but never pursued it, so I hope this book shows her that anything is possible, if you put your mind to it. She also helped me to get this book off the ground by helping to fund it, so for that I am greatly indebted (in every sense of the word).

I would like to thank my two children Theodore and Athena who inspired the poems in my Blood, S*** and Tears chapter. Motherhood has certainly been a rollercoaster of a journey; not all good and not all bad either. You have both taught me so much about myself, being your mom has shown me how strong and compassionate I can be...and how easily manipulated I am when the waterworks start.

I would like to thank my husband Alex, who despite not getting all this "poetry stuff" has manned the fort whilst I've been doing events for the business and doing open mic nights; even tagging along to my events when he can, although it's not his thing.

I would like to thank my brother Mark for being my proof reader and for being so quick to get my work back to me so I could continue making progress. And thank you to Rebecca for all of your advice regarding fonts and alignment, it was a minefield but you helped me through by answering my many questions.

Thank you to Rebecca, Jay, Jemima and Spoz for taking the time to review this book and encouraging me to stop procrastinating and just get it published already. You are all an inspiration. The speak your mind events hosted by Jemima and the Word Association have really helped boost my confidence with sharing my poetry and had allowed me to meet more like-minded people like the wonderful Daniel Kay who after only having met me once started to send me inspirational messages each morning because he is the most kind and wonderful person I've had the pleasure of meeting. Thank you to the wonderful Worcester Lit fest and Fringe and all the other incredible open mic opportunities I've had both online and in person. Thank you in advance to all the venues and businesses that have allowed me to come and promote my poetry both on and offline. I really appreciate you letting me come into your space to share my message.

Thank you to the wonderfully talented Becky Hemsley and Kelly the Poet for answering all of my many questions on how to get a book self published. I was completely out of my depth and didn't know where to start. Becky in particular you have been golden, even answering questions about font sizes....FONT SIZES! I wish you every success for all of your amazing poetry books released and yet to be released.

I also want to give a huge shoutout to Canva where this book has been designed through. It truly is a fantastic design app that opens up all opportunities to creatives.

Thank you to Home-Start North-East Worcestershire who have helped to support me through my battles with Post-Natal Depression and beyond. They are an incredible charity who do incredible work, so please if you can make a donation to them please do so they can continue to help support vulnerable families.

And finally thank you to you! The person who has bought and read this book and made a dream of mine come true. You are the reason I wanted to share these poems in the first place, and I hope they have given you comfort, made you smile, made you laugh and made you feel that you are not alone.

Natalie xxx

THINGS TO HELP YOU WITH YOUR OWN MENTAL HEALTH

Body scan
Move your attention to different areas of the body, starting from top or bottom. Where do you feel warm? where do you feel tension? where do you feel relaxed?

Mindful colouring and drawing
Focus on the colours and the sensation of drawing rather than the drawing itself.

Take notice
Take notice of your feelings and validate yourself for feeling them.

Question your reaction
Question your reactions to feelings if you need to. "I understand why you are angry as that person nearly hit your car, how could you channel that anger in a safe way?"

Make time for mindfulness, set it as part of your routine, take it slowly and be kind to yourself.
Use Apps such as Calm and create playlists that you can listen to that help keep you balanced. Music makes a huge impact on mental wellbeing.

CHARITIES TO CONTACT
Maternal Mental Health and family support
Home-Start: 0116 464 5490, info@home-start.org.uk
Sure Start: 0121 552 9248
Starting well: 01905 760000, startingwellworcs.nhs.uk

Mental Health Charities
Papyrus Helpline: 0800 068 4141
Mind Infoline: 0300 123 3393
Anxiety UK Helpline: 03444 775 774
CALM helpline (Campaign Against Living Miserably): 0800 585858
Samaritans helpline: 116-123
Together for Mental Wellbeing helpline: 020 7780 7300

MINDFULNESS ACTIVITY

If you need to take some time out or you are feeling overwhelmed, this activity will help to ground you. It will help you to focus on what is happening in the moment and what your next step could be.

STAND UP AND BREATHE.

Feel your **connection** to the earth

TUNE INTO YOUR BODY.

Lower your gaze. Scan your body and **notice** physical sensations or emotions. Discharge unpleasant **sensations**, emotions or feelings on the out breath. **Notice** any pleasant ones and let them fill you up.

OBSERVE

Lift your eyes and take in your surroundings. **Observe** something in your environment that is pleasant and be **grateful** for it and its beauty.

POSSIBILITY

Ask yourself what is **possible** or what is new or what is a **forward** step.

If you find yourself being reactive , try the following...

PAUSE AND TAKE ONE TO THREE BIG BREATHES

"step back" (you don't have to physically step back just in your mind)

"Clear head"

"Calm body"

BREATHE AGAIN

"Relax", "melt" or "ease"

MINDFULNESS OBSERVATIONS

This is a great exercise that can be done with your children too. If you are feeling anxious; focus on your senses. When we become really attuned to what is happening around us, we can use this as a distraction to help bring ourselves down from a state of panic. The more often we do this, the more it will become second nature. The more specific we can get, the better the outcome of the exercise. You could then possibly use your observations to write poetry or prose; a great outlet for those suffering with mental health difficulties.

Notice **FIVE THINGS THAT YOU CAN** *SEE...*
Things that you wouldn't normally notice, like a shadow or a crack.

Notice **FOUR THINGS THAT YOU CAN** *FEEL...*
The texture of your clothes on your skin, the breeze, smooth surface of a table.

Notice **THREE THINGS THAT YOU CAN** *HEAR...*
It could be the chirp of a bird, the hum of the fridge, a dripping tap or the subtle sound of traffic.

Notice **TWO THINGS THAT YOU CAN** *SMELL...*
Whether they are pleasant or unpleasant, bring them into focus. The smell of a flower or of food cooking.

Notice **ONE THING THAT YOU CAN** *TASTE...*
Take a sip of a drink, chew a piece of chewing gum, notice the taste in your mouth and how the taste makes you feel.

Printed in Great Britain
by Amazon

49364512R00165